Before Modern Conveniences

One Finnish Farm Family 1917–1927

Helmi Kortes-Erkkila
Illustrated by her daughter, Lynne Meier

HATS OFF

Helmi Kortes-Erkkila

**Before Modern Conveniences:
One Finnish Farm Family 1917–1927**

Copyright © 2004 Helmi Kortes-Erkkila
Illustrations copyright © 2004 Lynne Meier

All rights reserved. No part of this book may be reproduced or transmitted in any form or by any means without the written consent of the publisher.

Published by Hats Off Books™
610 East Delano Street, Suite 104
Tucson, Arizona 85705

ISBN: 1-58736-271-6
LCCN: 2003097293

TABLE OF CONTENTS

Introduction 1
1 Alone with a Kitten 3
2 Food on the Kitchen Table 15
3 Health Customs and Reliable Cures 29
4 U.S. Mail: Our Connection to the Outside World . . .47
5 Visitors: Friends and Salesmen 61
6 Work: Part of Daily Living 71
7 The Games We Played 91
8 School Days 109
9 The Finn Hall: Our Community Center 139
10 I'm a Teenager! 163

Suggested Topics for Thought, Discussion or
Written Assignment 169

ILLUSTRATIONS

Kitten Comfort 5
A Boy's Bare Bottom 7
Fantasy Carving 10
Dancing at Beauty Spot 19
A Tanned Shaved Head 33
Relieving Papa's Back 37
Dr. Hoffman 41
Sick 43
World War I Was Over 48
Making a Cake 51
Drawing Me 64

A Broken Dish 73
Working and Dancing 76
Helping in the Barn 77
Plowing to Plant Potatoes 83
Filling the Wood Box 85
Changing Routine of Cows 89
Crashing through the Kitchen Window 92
Musical Evening at Home 95
London Bridge 99
Ballet Dancers 103
Limited Sharing 114
Unusual Bird in the Sky 118
Pot-Bellied Stove at the Co-op Store 121
Weeding Aunt's Flowers 125
Slow Wagon Ride 128
Learned Obedience 134
Whose Papa is Santa? 141
Knitting Christmas Presents 144
Reading Becomes Learning 153
Women Express Opinions 156
Finn Hall Music 159
Dancing with Jeff 161

Introduction

The intent of this book is to acquaint the youth of today with what people did before they had modern conveniences. Family life consisted of arduous physical work, distributed according to strength and age, with moments of relaxation and togetherness. Modern conveniences such as electricity, dishwashers, vacuum cleaners, hair dryers, telephones, radios, television, and computers were unknown. Automobiles were in use by a few, but none in this community.

Each chapter concentrates on a particular subject but includes Miriami's fantasies and flashbacks.

These were the golden years of American farm life before the Great Depression, which caused discord and problems nationally as well as locally. The author's parents settled in Cowlitz County, southwest Washington State, on 40 wooded acres in the foothills of the town of Woodland, which lies upriver from the confluence of the Lewis and the Columbia. The events are not necessarily in chronological order, but they all took place. With the exception of a few well-known individuals in the community, names of Finnish characters are fictional.

From the sponge of time, certain special events trickle into the writer's memory. The lives of her parents differed from those of most Finnish settlers. Her father was one of two Finns in Woodland who was a citizen. He had participated in the Hibbing, Minnesota, strike of 1907 and was blacklisted along with all the other miners. Unable to get a job, he enlisted as a student at the *Työväenopisto* (Work People's College) in Minnesota. He studied English and various college subjects to qualify for citizenship. He met his future wife, the author's mother, while she was a dishwasher at the college. Prior to that, she had worked in several newly wealthy homes where she had picked up a smattering of ideas of what it was like to be an American, much of which she insisted be put into effect in her own life.

Apart from a small one-room structure set up as a church by fewer than half a dozen families, there was only one community center in the area: the Finn hall. More than fifty families participated in activities there. All conversations at the hall and at the home of the author were in Finnish. Consequently, although her father spoke English when it was necessary for business, the author made no attempt to improvise a broken English accent as she seldom heard any uttered.

The Woodland Finnish settlers were scattered over several hilly areas quite a distance from each other. The hall, centrally located, was a convenient place for them to gather. This ethnic group debated the social and economic problems they faced, thus absorbing democratic values via the stream of local events and nationally from their newspapers.

From her experiences at the hall and the common language that held the community together, the author learned that people of different political, religious, and social backgrounds could get along with each other. Since it was a formative period for her, she believes it may set a practical lesson for people today.

1

Alone with a Kitten

Mama comforted me. That was unusual of her. "Yes, you may get one of the kittens from the nest." She added, "The mother cat won't be there. I'm sure she's gone hunting. The kittens are old enough to be away from their mother for a few hours." I heard her call, "Hurry back," as I skipped to the makeshift barn.

With Mama's words following me, I had my mind's eye on the kittens. I knew which one I wanted: the firstborn, like my sister, who was born two years before me and got all sorts of privileges. That wasn't fair, but it would be OK with a firstborn kitten; kittens weren't people. Whenever Mama looked at me, she always said, "No, no, no," but today she had actually given me permission to pick a kitten to stay with me while she walked to town! That made me happy. Woodland was many miles away, but I wouldn't be alone; I would have a kitten for company!

I remembered watching the mama cat give birth. My eyes were glued to the first one that slid from her body. It was white with black spots on its closed eyes and on its back and belly. The tip of the tail was also black. I remembered how shocked I was at seeing the mama cat's belly bulge and then contract as, one after the other, more kittens slowly came into view. At the same time she was licking the first one's face and body. By giving more attention to the firstborn, she was acting just like Mama, who pandered to my sister, Helvi, but always found something I did that she didn't like.

When I got to the barn, the mama cat wasn't there. The kittens lay with their legs flung over each other. It was not difficult to find my special kitten. Untangling its body from the other five, I picked it up carefully and raised it to my face. It was warm and soft. While caressing it, I murmured, "Kitty-kitty-kitty" and ignored the others. This was the kitty I wanted to stay with me while Mama was away.

Despite Mama's command to hurry back, I walked as slowly as I dared. I did not really like to be left alone at home even with a kitten to keep me company. The slower I walked, the longer Mama would be at home. Helvi was at school. Papa was working for Mountain Timber Company and only came home late Saturdays. He cleared trees on the farm until late Sunday afternoon. Now Mama was going to walk many, many miles to town and would be gone for a long time. She was leaving me alone with my kitten.

As I entered the room, Mama threw a scarf over her head and came to the kitten cradled in my hands. Without glancing at me, she patted the kitty and said, "Take good care of Spotty." She had named my kitty! It just snuggled in my hands, but I was annoyed. I cared. I wanted to name the kitty! Mama had named both Helvi and me because Papa had been working in a gold mine in Nevada when Helvi was born and in a copper mine in Idaho when I was born. Of course, it was a Mama's right to name the kids when papas were away, but my feelings were hurt because I wanted to name Spotty. The name fit. Why hadn't I thought of it?!

Daydreaming with my furry friend Spotty snuggled in my hands, I heard Mama instructing me. Her advice seemed to come from far away. I heard something like, "Don't leave the house." After a pause I heard, "Don't put wood in the stove." Then came, "It's going to be warm today so you won't get cold." Somewhere mixed in the list of do-nots, I heard there was bread, butter and milk in the pantry if I got hungry. I was always hungry; she knew that! Looking up, I saw she was no longer in the kitchen. She had left me all alone with Spotty.

I dragged a kitchen chair into the bedroom and placed it near the window facing the trail where Mama sped along on her errand. I sat down with Spotty and was warmed by the morning sun and comforted by Spotty on my lap.

Mama was getting dynamite from the co-op for Papa so he could blow up tree stumps and clear land for a hay field. Mama wanted to have more cows and they needed to eat hay to make milk. It cost a lot of money to buy hay so Papa worked away from our farm to have our own hay fields.

Everything cost money, except having kittens. The mama cat was given milk every morning and evening and the kittens wrestled with each other as they suckled milk from her many nipples. The mama cat got most of her food from hunting mice. She liked to eat them. That didn't make her fat. She got fat because she had a belly full of kittens. That was like having a baby; women got that way, too. I didn't want to have a baby. I remembered how the mama cat was in pain having the kittens. If I got big and heavy like cats and mamas, could I run errands like I did now?

I knew babies came from mothers' tummies. Mama's sister Sanni knew everything because her husband had gone to college and worked in a Finnish newspaper in Astoria. She told us about the birds and bees. Birds were like chickens and laid eggs. The eggs inside the hen were fertilized by roosters, which just jumped on the hind ends of chickens now and then. When the hen was in the mood to have baby chicks, she sat on the eggs she had laid and warmed them for days and days with her feathery body until the chicks pecked their way out of the shell and said, "Peep-peep." That was their way of saying, "Here I am!" Baby chicks looked like kittens when they were born—moist and sickly looking until the feathers got fluffy, just like the kitten's fur became soft and silky.

A few weeks earlier we had stopped by to greet our neighbors who had just moved to Butte Hill. Wilho, their son, had invited me to see something special behind his home. What could a new boy on the hill show me that was special? I was curious so I followed him eagerly. After he ran around the corner of the house, he quickly turned around, bent forward, pulled down his trousers and laughed. I saw his behind! Was he playing rooster and had he put a seed into me like

Aunt Sanni had said? The thought of having a baby worried me. Frightened, I ran into the house and clung to Mama.

Caught up in the steady chitchat of the new neighbor lady, Mama barely noticed me. Holding a cup of coffee, she finally asked quite casually what the matter was. I sobbed, "I want to go home." She must have thought I was tired. I did not tell her how frightened and worried I was. I thought there was a connection between Wilho's bare bottom and what I saw roosters do to chickens. I never did tell anyone what Wilho did. I worried about it for a long time.

Momentarily aware of the kitten and warmed by the sun, I comforted the bundle of fur on my lap. It occasionally shifted position. I think it liked being with me even though I wasn't its mama. Once in a while I looked out the window and saw the trail Mama had taken. I expected her to get home before my sister, Helvi, arrived home from school. The school bus drove the students all the way eastward on Lewis River Road and let the kids off at the foot of Butte Hill Road. Then they had to walk two miles uphill to get home. Usually Helvi was tired and hungry when she arrived. I wanted to play school with her, but she wanted to eat, not play. She never wanted to do what I wanted. Maybe all sisters were like that. It would have been different if I'd been a boy; Mama would have liked me better. I wouldn't have gotten in her way.

While the kitten was rearranging itself on my lap, I thought of the time our house was being built. That was a long, long time ago. A neighbor helped Papa. There were scraps of sawed-off lumber here and there. I picked up a chunk and asked Papa for something with which to carve. Sitting on a slope with my legs dangling, I spent the afternoon carving a horse.

When Papa and the other men got together, all they talked about was horses. Horses did all the hard work on farms, pulling plows while men pushed the blade deep into the ground and steered to make straight furrows. I knew that pulling was much harder than pushing. Even I could push someone down, but I couldn't pull that person so horses were much stronger than men. Since we didn't have a horse, I enjoyed carving one for our farm.

Mama said Finnish girls didn't work with horses; they just took care of cows. Cows were not as pretty as horses. Cows had curved and dangerous horns, but horses had straight, long tails and hair that flipped and flopped—just like mine, except my hair was curly. Horses had soft lips and powerful flanks that were wiped clean by their tails. Even if there were no flies around, they whisked their tails right and left. When they did that, one could see what strong muscles they had.

While carving my horse, I realized that horses ate more hay than cows because they were bigger and stronger. We sure needed hay fields.

Papa used a scythe to cut grass from a meadow near our house so we had hay for the cow that was tethered nearby. Mama milked the cow, but Papa kept talking about getting a horse. Without its work, he couldn't make fields and we needed to have two cows. A cow that has a calf in its belly doesn't give milk for a while because the calf, just before it's born, needs nourishment. If we'd had two cows, we'd have had milk all the time. I had never seen a calf born, but I thought it hurt the cow just like it did mama cats.

If I were a boy, I thought, I'd grow up to be a man. Then I could be a papa. I thought being a papa was better than being a mama. Papa never bossed me like Mama did. He didn't boss Helvi either, but that's because she didn't make mistakes. She wasn't curious like me. so she didn't get into trouble. Helvi was in school now while I was sitting alone with Spotty. I didn't think it was fair that she was learning while I was just sitting and thinking. Mama said I was too young to go to school. I knew better. I could learn more at school than at home.

I wondered when Mama would be back from town. I remembered how nice she'd been to me that day long ago, the day after I had carved the horse and couldn't find it. I cried really hard. I cried so hard the men stopped bending over the two-by-fours they were putting in place for the frame of our house. Mama, who had been puttering around the construction site, came to me and asked what was wrong. I told her I couldn't find the horse I'd carved. She smiled gently, put her arms around me, and pressed me to her soft tummy. That felt good. Mama spoke slowly, "Maybe your horse went looking for a stable." After a moment she added, "Everyone needs a home, so it just galloped away."

Mama had understood! Everyone needed a home to live in, even horses, and I had carelessly left it lying down on the grass when I had left for the day. Chickens lived in coops, cows in barns, pigs in pens, horses in stables. My horse must have gone in search of a stable!

Shifting the chair slightly as the sun rays changed, I wondered if it was right for me to keep Spotty away from its mama's care, but Mama had told me not to leave the house so I couldn't take it back. I wondered if Mama knew cats as well as she knew cows. I thought our mama cat would want her kittens in the nest she had made for them with her paws. Grown-ups knew more than kids, but I felt more than Mama because I had never seen her cry. I cried a lot, but I felt better afterwards. I didn't know why.

Spotty had fallen asleep and I kept gazing through the window at the path where I would see Mama returning. I

Before Modern Conveniences

thought how nice it would be to be a boy because then Papa would let me work with him. Boys were allowed to curry horses, but girls had to brush cows' coats. They often had dried manure on their flanks. I could see the dust drip when Mama brushed our cow. If I had manure on my clothes, Mama would wash them. First she would scold me in disgust.

When Papa was home, he was always outdoors except for eating, drinking coffee and sleeping. With the help of a neighbor, he had cut down a lot of trees. The noise of the saw was different from people talking. When the trees fell, they made a crashing sound. It was louder than Papa's coughing and louder than people applauding at the Finn hall. Papa cut trees for two reasons: to get a big supply of wood for the stove to keep us warm during the winter and for Mama to use to cook our food. Now Mama had gone to get something for Papa to blow up the stumps. Our farm didn't look at all like it had when we had first moved in. It had a scattering of stumps all over the slopes that now had to be removed.

Men changed the world: anyone could see that. I would have liked to have been a boy and grown up to be a man. Then I would have changed the world by making hay fields so everyone would have plenty of milk and butter. Nobody would have been hungry if I had my way.

Spotty began to stretch its legs and move slowly on my lap. I knew how boys differed from girls. We were not alike when naked. I knew: I had seen a few boys in the sauna. I became curious. Was Spotty a boy or a girl? Parting its hind legs, I saw Spotty was a she. Someday she'd get as fat as her mama had been. Maybe I would get fat if Wilho had put a seed in me. I liked taking care of a kitten but not a baby!

With Spotty crawling up my chest, I shifted the chair to another spot in line with the sunlight from the other window in the room. I wished Mama would come back. I hoped she wasn't like the horse I'd carved that went off to another place because we didn't have a stable. Mama just had to come back: Papa was coming home the following night and he needed what she was buying. Spotty began crawling all over my lap. Maybe she wanted her mama; I was worried about mine. I didn't like to be alone too long. Mama had been away for a long time already.

Then, far off in the distance, a head came into view. Maybe it was Mama. I was so excited I got halfway up from the chair but sat down right away. Although I wanted to run out to meet her, I just sat cuddling Spotty and waited. She had told me not to go out of the house. I would show her that I knew how to obey! Spotty kept my hands busy. She was crawling all over. It was hard to keep her on my lap.

The figure was in full view now: I saw it was Mama! About time. I was very tired of sitting and waiting. Even Spotty needed her mama now. I would tell Mama I hadn't gone out of the house—not once!

Entering the house with her usual firm footsteps, Mama carefully placed a package on the kitchen table. It was wrapped in brown paper and bound securely with string. She took off her scarf with a sigh of relief. "Been a good girl?" She expected me to be good even though she usually thought I wasn't. I muttered, "I sat here the whole time you were away," and then burst into tears. She comforted me with a quick hug, saying, "Mirri, take Spotty back to her nest. Her mother must be looking for her." She called me by that pet name only when she was pleased with me.

Spotty clung to my chest as I left. Mama had not told me to hurry, as she usually did, so I just walked slowly. I would have liked to have had Spotty with me all day. Mama would say it was wrong and Papa would say the kitty would die from lack of food, but it felt good to think that I could somehow keep Spotty with me—maybe when she was a grown-up cat. I knew Mama would not let any cat live in the house. Cats belonged in the barn where they could catch mice.

When I arrived at the cat's nest, the mama cat looked comfortable as she lay with the litter of five asleep next to her belly. She moved slightly, muttered a low guttural sound of contentment and stretched her body as Spotty clambered over her sleeping pals and began to suck. She was hungry. She pawed her mama's tummy just like all the others had done. I had not taught them that. It was what kittens did naturally. Papa said it was kitten culture.

I had to leave them. Helvi would be home from school anytime. I had forgotten to eat anything while Mama was gone. I was as hungry as Spotty. Mama and food were in the kitchen.

2

Food on the Kitchen Table

I knew Mama would have something to eat on the table because Helvi would be arriving. Even if Papa wasn't home, I hoped Mama would have her usual afternoon cup of coffee. I liked that because it was a time we three were together and Mama wasn't working.

While loitering and thinking of Spotty, I saw Helvi coming down the ridge. Smoke was flowing from the chimney. I hoped Mama had not yet had her coffee and gone to work in the fields. I ran to get to the house before Helvi did. I liked to be first at some things, especially since I was younger. Mama was in the house. What a relief!

I had no sooner plopped myself on a chair by the table than Helvi came in carrying a book. A book! Several days earlier I had peeked at her book. I could read a few words that Helvi had pointed out to me. I imagined what the story was about and spoke English out loud: "Jibber-jabber-dabber." That was how English sounded, but I knew what I was saying. I was an English teacher!

My mind snapped from the fantasy to the display of food on the table. Two glasses of milk and some cardamom biscuits lay there. A much used, soot-covered pot was set in the removable section of the stove lid. That way the water boiled faster because it was in direct contact with fire. When the water boiled, Mama poured it over the grounds in the coffee pot. In order to settle the grounds, she moved the pot to a cooler place on top of the stove for a while.

Helvi put her book aside and sat down across the table from me. We both dug into the cardamom biscuits and drank our milk. The milk was fresh, this morning's offering from our cow. It was neither cold nor warm, but just right—like the temperature outside. Papa had cut a small hole next to the ceiling in the pantry and another near ground level. That way, he said, the outside air would circulate in the pantry. Mama was afraid that mice or insects would get in so Papa hammered a fly screen over both holes.

If the weather was hot, the milk would sour and Mama would put something into it to make *viiliä*, which was like yogurt. When the milk had set, we would eat the *viiliä* with a spoon. Sometimes we sprinkled a little sugar and cinnamon on top. That tasted really good.

Today's milk, however, was not sour. We gulped it down after sampling the cardamom delicacy. Mama sat at the table with us, enjoying her coffee. She had poured thick cream on top that had turned the coffee the color of mud. The cream was kept in the pantry.

Papa had not planned to build a pantry; he had expected to build shelves on the kitchen wall where dishes and food could be put, but Mama had seen that the American women where she worked as a maid had pantries and clothes closets. She had observed the American style of living so she insisted on having a pantry and a clothes closet when our house was built. Even though all the other Finns built a sauna in which to live before their houses were built, Mama talked Papa into building a house first. We went to the neighbors on Saturday nights to take our baths. The men always had their bath first and talked farming and politics. After bathing, I didn't listen to their talk. I was sleepy and tired after the hot and sweaty sauna.

I was chewing slowly because my mind had wandered, so Helvi was through eating before I was. In accordance with Mama's instructions, she changed into her everyday clothes and hung her school dress on a nail in the closet. Gulping the last of the milk, I called to her, "Let's play school!" She pretended she hadn't heard, so I shouted, "I want to be the teacher!" In her matter-of-fact voice, Helvi replied that she had other plans. "Besides," she added, "I'm older than you. I should be the teacher."

The very idea of Helvi being the teacher was silly. She didn't like school as much as I did. When Helvi was in the second grade, she invited me to school with her one day. I watched what the teacher did. At times I thought I could understand what she said. Mama had constantly told me to watch how she did something: that was how one learned. Helvi didn't watch. She had her nose in a book. Maybe she was reading. I wished I could read. I would have liked to talk like teachers, not in Finnish.

I didn't think Mama had been listening to us girls. Having had her coffee, she changed into her work clothes and ordered me to go with her to milk the cow. Mama informed Helvi that we were going to have potato chowder for dinner. She told her to peel some potatoes and put them into a pot with a cut-up onion and a few kernels of pepper, then barely cover them with water from a bucket on the bench outside on the porch. When the potatoes were soft enough, Helvi was to add a cupful of milk. Mama warned Helvi not to put the lid back on the pot because the milk would come to a boil and flow all over the stove, making a mess. When we ate chowder, we were allowed to sprinkle a little salt or pepper on it. Mama raised her voice when she said the word little. Salt and pepper cost a lot of money. In addition to the chowder, we were to have a glassful of milk and several slices of graham flour bread with lots of butter.

After several days Mama would make a pudding from any leftover cardamom biscuits. She cut the leftovers into chunks and soaked them in a mixture of egg and milk. They were then baked in the oven until solid. I liked it. We didn't have dessert often, usually only when Papa was home. The cardamom pudding was special.

I liked to hear Papa talk and smoke his pipe after eating. Papa thought the smoke from the pipe would dry the drip from his nose and stop his cough. He coughed a lot to clear his lungs of the mine dust that had settled there. After eating, Mama and Papa talked about work. That was their favorite subject.

I was often asked to run errands. Mama liked it when I dashed here and there, bringing things to her or taking them away. I thought I would become a runner. Papa said the very best athletes took part in the Olympics. Maybe I could be an Olympian! I tried not to waste a second when asked to run errands. Although no one told me, I knew I was good at that.

Sometime later in the summer Mama and Papa decided it would be a good idea to have a Butte Hill picnic on the ridge above the house. The picnic would be held beneath a huge maple tree with branches spreading over a wide area. The grass had not grown much underneath the tree so it was a perfect gathering place.

The first time I was able to coax Helvi up there, she took one look and exclaimed, "What a beautiful spot!" I felt like dancing and flinging my arms so I did. From then on we called it our beauty spot. Helvi didn't dance in joy as I did. She just gave me a quick glance and stooped to pick a handful of dandelions for Mama. Dandelions are bright yellow and round like the sun, but they have no fragrance. Mama didn't mind.

She put them into a pint mason jar with water from the bucket on the porch.

I heard Papa tell Mama, "The best place for a good field is up there on top of the ridge." He added, "That means the big maple tree has to come down." That's when Mama made the suggestion to invite all Butte Hillers to a picnic before Papa cut down the tree and got rid of the brush nearby. I thought Mama made the suggestion so she would meet people of her own age. Was she tired of having me hang around her all the time? She often looked disgusted at what I had done and then repeated the job herself. I didn't like that.

A picnic was something new for everyone. It was not to be our beauty spot any more; instead it was to be a gathering place for the neighbors. I did not like the idea of losing my dancing spot, but I was told our cow's need for hay was more important than my wanting to dance up there.

I wanted to practice Olympics by running to tell all the families about the picnic, but Papa had told the clerk at the co-op to inform the folks on our hill about it. She was as good as her promise. Everyone came and enjoyed our beauty spot.

It was exciting to watch Papa set up the table for the food that the people brought with them. Of course, there was no real table. Papa placed a wide rough board between two sawhorses. The women spread dish towels on the board and then placed food on it. It looked like a real celebration was to take place.

I had never seen so much food at one time—all kinds of color. There was food I had never seen before. Helvi named everything as we stalked up one side of the long table and down the other side. She pointed to the green tomato relish and cucumber pickles; squeaky yellowish cheese; white potato salad; red beet salad dotted with bits of herring; transparent headcheese spotted with gray shreds of meat; pink slices of salted salmon; several containers of bright yellow butter; and round, square and rectangular loaves of bread. Somebody had brought two jugs of buttermilk, which held down the flapping dish towels at each end of the table.

Helvi and I were not the only kids pushing and shoving one another as we gawked at all the food. Above the chatter and excitement, Mama called, "Children, get plates and utensils from your mothers and fill your plates!"

We heard! We stopped gawking at the food and ran to get plates from the outstretched hands of our mothers. We took a little of everything and filled our plates. It was exciting and new to all of us. With a cup of buttermilk in one hand and an overflowing plate in the other, we scuffled our way to the other side of the maple tree. Sitting cross-legged on the ground with my plate on my lap, I ate hurriedly. Everything tasted better because this was a picnic.

The grown-ups wasted no time in filling their plates and proceeded to eat either sitting down or lying on their sides on the ground. Finally, as Finns do, somebody complained there was no coffee. With a loud guffaw, a man bellowed, "The old lady fixed up some coffee in my thermos!" He added that he did not have enough to share with the other men in the group. I saw his wife wince when she heard what he called her. She poked her friend and whispered that her husband was showing off because he was 10 years older than she. I heard Mama say to the woman next to her, "Too bad the rest of us didn't think of bringing coffee." She sighed and added, "My husband's thermos is gathering dust in the pantry. He hasn't used it since he got hurt in the the woods."

The men and women sat separately in small groups talking to one another. After refilling their plates and a lot of chatter, the women began to gather and sort what was left on the table. The picnic was over. Someone ordered the men to stop smoking and to start for home. Evening chores were facing everyone. Nobody went home hungry. I went to sleep that evening thinking of the picnic feast at our beauty spot. I had lost the special place where I could dance on top of the ridge of my world, but I understood why.

One day Mama was surprised to see Leppänen, a family friend who lived down by Lewis River, walking slowly down the path from the ridge with a gunny sack on his back. Mama got excited and immediately ordered me to get the coffee grinder. She poured the beans into the cup on top and told me to get busy. I did. I liked to see Mama happy as Leppänen came into the house. He lowered his voice. "Never mind the off-season, here's food for the family." After a pause he added, "People have to eat, law or no law." Mama nodded. After drinking his coffee, he left with a dollar donated by

Mama from her big black leather purse. He had to hurry home to do some more fishing while the run was good.

When one touches a fish, it is slimy. I didn't ever want to be a fisherman or a butcher, even if they provided food for people, but I liked to see Mama clean scales from the salmon and wash and gut the fish. Helvi was at school so she didn't get to see the insides of the fish. Mama put them aside for the cats. She cut the fish into many different shapes. Some she cut into strips. She let me help her put rock salt at the bottom of the crock, between and above each layer of the strips. When the crock was full, Mama placed a clean board over the contents and a heavy rock on top of it. The fish would be made into casseroles during the winter. That evening, however, we had fish chowder, which we called *kala mojakka*.

Papa jokingly told Mama that she should put the eyes of the fish into the chowder. Chuckling in his quiet way, he said that with fish eyes staring at us, we wouldn't eat so much of this special treat. Mama shot right back that growing kids had to eat. She didn't realize that Papa was joking. She added that she would feel guilty with fish eyes floating on top of the chowder gazing at her, but we had heard that Tauno's mama enjoyed eating fish eyes because they tasted good. That's how different people were, even though they were neighbors and grown-ups.

Papa butchered a pig, but he didn't want me to see him killing it. Afterwards we didn't call it pig meat; it was called pork. The pork was something else to eat other than salted fish. Mama did the same with the pork as with the salmon. Another big crock was filled with slabs of pork, surrounded by and covered with rock salt. During the winter it was a change to have slices of salt pork fried golden brown in a cast-iron frying pan and brown gravy made out of flour and potato water instead of boiled potatoes or a salt-fish casserole.

For a couple of days after Papa had butchered a pig, we ate better than at the beauty spot picnic. We had pork chops fried light brown and mashed potatoes covered with gravy made from the frying-pan fat. At these times there was no conversation. We all enjoyed the chops. Seeing how absorbed we were, Papa joked, "Even if we're eating pork chops, we don't have to eat like pigs." None of us paid attention to his remark. We kept gnawing as close to the bone as possible to clean off all the meat. Despite his joking, Papa gnawed like we all did. I didn't deny we were eating like pigs, but I thought we were gnawing the bones more like dogs.

Once in a while Mama thought we had too many roosters. I saw her butcher one. She laid the rooster on a big chopping block near the chicken coop, held its feet in one hand and chopped off the head. Then she threw the headless rooster onto the ground. I saw it flapping its wings as it struggled on the ground. Mama said it wasn't alive any more so I was not to be concerned; it didn't feel anything. Mama said its muscles had not received the message that it was dead. It looked like a battle for life. Or was the body trying to find the head? I was horrified.

After plucking off the feathers and removing the insides, she dressed the rooster by stuffing it before she put it into the oven. The stuffing was a mixture of bread, onion and seasoning that was put into the carcass where the guts had been. When I dressed myself, I put my clothes on, but when Mama dressed the bird, it was cooking language.

For some reason Mama thought hens tasted a little bit better than roosters so she always fixed roast chicken for Helvi and me during the holiday season. That was the time that she and Papa had their favorite food of the year, a *lipeäkala* (*lutefisk*) dinner, like in the old country. Mama always invited friends to share the meal. Helvi and I would not eat *lutefisk*. When it was being cooked, the house smelled awful. It was not quite like the smell of a skunk but stinky in another way. After a meal, the forks, knives and spoons turned black. I convinced Mama that it might also turn the insides of our stomachs black, so that's why she killed a chicken to roast just for us two.

Helvi thanked me for getting Mama to fix a roast chicken. Mama said she didn't mind because she knew how to pick out a chicken that wasn't laying eggs. She watched the hens well but didn't name them like she named each of our five cows. We had 40 chickens. That was too many to name; besides, they all looked exactly alike.

One Thanksgiving Day when Mama was cleaning a hen for the holiday, she groaned, "My, oh, my, I made a mistake. It would have been laying many eggs soon!" That's when I realized that she could misjudge chickens just like she misjudged me.

I enjoyed holiday meals because Papa didn't work in the fields. He liked company, just like the rest of us did. On holidays, grown-ups didn't talk about farming or politics. While spooning some of Mama's white sauce over the boiled potatoes and *lutefisk*, the men spoke of old country memories. They laughed and shoved food into their mustache-decorated mouths, smacked their lips, and remarked how good the gravy was. Mama had boiled a few eggs, cut them up into small pieces and then dumped them into a flour-and-milk mixture while adding salt, pepper and other seasoning.

On this occasion the *lutefisk* was well done but firm as it should be. "Just like old times in Finland" was heard from the dining room while Helvi and I were digging into the roast chicken in the kitchen. Although nobody mentioned anything about the taste of the fish, they ate it all. Helvi and I couldn't eat the entire roast chicken. The next day our family had the rest of the real American food. I thought both Papa and Mama liked it better than what they had had the day before.

Eventually we had five cows and two horses. Our fields couldn't produce enough hay to have any more animals. Whenever a cow calved, Mama made a special pudding with the fresh milk that was supposed to be fed to the newly born calf. What was left over was poured into a quart bottle. Mama instructed me, "Run to Tauno's home, Miriami, and hand this jar to his mother." Deciding that wasn't enough information, she continued, "Tell her that this is the first milking after our cow freshened."

Everybody knew that kind of milk was good for one's health and Tauno's mother was delighted with the gift. Actually it wasn't a gift; it was repayment for the milk she had sent us when their cow had freshened. This custom dated way back to the days when they were in the old country. I liked it. It gave me a chance to run as well as visit with Tauno. Talking to him was not like talking to girls, but that was OK: I could pretend I was a boy.

Bread was the staff of life in our family. Even after eating our cooked oatmeal in the mornings, we had a slice of bread and butter. Bread was eaten at every meal, including an extra chunk with which to clean our plates.

After kneading bread dough by hand for a long time, Mama cut it up into sections and put it into rectangular bread pans, but sometimes she made a round loaf to lay on the grates. That made the crust hard. Helvi and I enjoyed chewing the crust when it was spread with lots of our homemade butter. Some Finns sold all their butter so the family didn't have any to put on their bread. Instead, they used bacon grease. That way they had money from the sale of butter to make the annual mortgage payment. We preferred to put butter on our bread and tried to save for the mortgage in other ways.

Everybody had a mortgage except rich people, but Mama said in America we were not going to eat as if we were dirt poor. She had been dirt poor in the old country because their one-room shack had a dirt floor. We had a floor made of Douglas fir planks that collected dust in the crevices. The dust was swept away so the floor wouldn't get dirty, but dust in the crevices was not the same as a dirt floor in the old country.

Even though pigs were dirty, I liked to eat pork chops, but I didn't like butchering and told Papa so. "That's life," Papa replied seriously with a sad look on his face. He added, "You'll understand when you're older." I didn't want to tell Papa that even kids could understand because that would sound as if I was arguing with him. I just knew killing was wrong—anyplace, anytime.

A catastrophe took place one fall. A blight hit our potato crop. The vines turned black and the potatoes, although underground, were black and soggy. Our basic food supply for the winter was gone! The root cellar would have no spuds in the bins. Helvi and I had learned that was what the American people called potatoes. The word "spud" didn't sound like "potato," but it was easier to say and spell. Shortcuts in words were OK, but I didn't take shortcuts when running. Running was easier than work. Maybe that's why I really enjoyed being on the go.

I heard Mama and Papa talk about what they should buy to take the place of the lost potato crop. It was decided that Papa should purchase a 100-pound sack of dried green peas from the co-op. Mama made pea soup for us all winter long. She soaked the dried peas overnight, cut a dry onion into bits, threw in some peppercorns and boiled the stuff together in a big pot. (Kids at school called almost everything "stuff" and I liked to speak like them.) Although we missed having potatoes at our meals, the pea soup was good. Along with Mama's bread, it was almost as good as eating mashed potatoes with brown gravy. That winter we sometimes had pancakes for supper with sugar and lots of butter. It was a change from pea soup.

At the dinner table Mama once wondered why Helvi and I had as many colds as kids who were allowed only skim milk at home. "We servants in Finland were allowed only skim milk to drink," she recalled. Looking at her, Papa said that skim milk had done well by her. He then added with a twinkle in his eye, "It's in the cards." Mama cringed for a moment and then shrugged it off. She thought playing cards was a waste of time. But I didn't think that's what Papa had in mind. I could tell from his eyes that what he had said had another meaning, but I didn't know what and I didn't ask. Papa was smart; he had gone to college. Besides, I had something more important to worry about.

Mama worried about the way I did almost everything, but my worry was about having a baby! It was real, just like the blight that had hit our potato crop, but nobody could see how worried I was. When I was busy running errands and pretending I was an Olympian, I was OK, though.

At our family coffee breaks, Helvi and I didn't always want to drink milk so we were allowed to have cambric tea. It was made from a cup filled with boiled water, a sprinkle of sugar and some milk. Papa said that's what Americans drank after they had the famous Boston Tea Party. However, we just called it "hot water" and enjoyed a cardamom biscuit with it.

None of my friends knew that drinking cambric tea was patriotic, but we didn't mind since we were promised a dollar at Christmas for not drinking coffee. Buying coffee beans cost money, so it was our way of saving to pay the mortgage! When we had out-of-town visitors, Helvi and I sat with the grown-ups and drank cambric tea while they had coffee at our kitchen table.

3

Health Customs and Reliable Cures

My parents had selected a flat area of ground below a slope for our house that was surrounded by three half-grown evergreen trees. When it was being built, we stayed at our neighbor's home about a mile away. Mama didn't want to bother the lady with our care while she helped Papa lay the foundations so she packed a lunch for all of us, and we spent the day with her and Papa.

Helvi tagged after Mama wherever she worked, but I seemed to be in everyone's way. Papa was hauling, lifting, bracing, and banging with a hammer on all shapes of wood. After playing with wood scraps, I realized I had to go potty, but there was nowhere to go. To get Mama's attention above the noise, I shouted, "I gotta go real bad!" This was followed by a more frantic yell from me, "But wheeeeeere?"

Before I realized what was happening, Mama had grabbed my hand and pulled me down the incline away from the construction work. "Pull down your pants and do your business," she ordered. From the sound of her voice, I could tell she would rather have been working with Papa. I was told to squat. It wasn't easy doing it while squatting. We were surrounded by large green ferns from which Mama plucked a handful of leaves and wiped my behind. I didn't like the squatting. I felt better, but Mama had other things on her mind than how I felt.

From the construction site, I heard Mama commanding Papa, "I want you to stop right now and do something more important!" Papa and a friend who was helping him stood frozen at the sound of her loud voice. Approaching them, she continued, "I want you to build an outside toilet."

"Whoever heard of building an outhouse before a house?" asked Papa's helper.

Mama raised her voice and spoke slowly. "I don't want my girls acting like animals. I want them to be civilized, like Americans." Catching her breath, she continued, "Never mind what other people have done. An outside toilet must be built!" This was followed by, "Now!"

Mama gave instructions on where she wanted the structure: halfway down the slope so only the upper part of the building would show from the house. Papa listened carefully and then gave orders to his helper. "Two holes, a large one for grown-ups and a smaller one for kids."

Mama interrupted. "Not too small; kids grow up very fast."

Papa did not dispute her advice. Picking lumber from scattered piles, the men started on the new structure. It was finished by the end of the day. Before trudging back to the neighbor's, we had already christened the new building. As the years went by, it became a place of refuge or escape for one reason or another, often from chores.

Papa worked from early morning until it was dark. We frequently stayed at the neighbor's house when Mama didn't have time to fix our lunch. Even if she wasn't a man, she knew how to do a man's work, like handling lumber. The outer frame of the house was finished when we moved into our new home. When inside, one could see two-by-fours, but that was OK. Mama nailed a calendar on one upright beam. Papa made a table from several planks and nailed the holder of a wall lamp directly above on another two-by-four. "So we'll be able to read at night," he said.

The summer was over. It was getting colder so we didn't like to go to the outhouse at night. A sturdy white porcelain pot was kept under Mama and Papa's bed. It was out of sight during the day. Sometimes when it was raining or snowing, both Helvi and I used it before going to bed. Mama didn't like that. She thought we should go to the outside toilet when we were still fully dressed. The potty, she claimed, was only for nighttime use. When we complained that it was cold or raining too hard to go outside, Mama sighed as we pulled our bloomers down and used the potty before putting on our flannel nightgowns. Mama emptied the contents from the potty every morning. (I didn't like the smell.) She rinsed it with water from a bucket that Papa had carried a long distance from the well.

When we had the money, Papa would lay galvanized pipes to the porch. We would then have gravity flow, which meant that we wouldn't need to buy a pump. Even though water didn't have legs like we did, Papa called it "running water." Having water piped to the porch would make housework easier. That would be better than in the old country and better than living with neighbors.

Mama instructed us to take care of our teeth properly by taking water from the bucket on the porch and rubbing salt on our gums, then rinsing out our mouths with water. We had to drink the rest of the water. It would be a waste to throw it away. I didn't like salt. Sometimes I didn't use any; I just swished the water in my mouth and spat it out. My teeth didn't know the difference and I sure wouldn't tell on myself.

When Papa bought toothbrushes for us from the co-op, Mama changed from salt to baking soda. I didn't like that either. Mama picked up ideas about cleaning teeth from the Finnish women's paper. She suggested that I read it and write to the children's corner. That would be something different from our usual activities, maybe even fun.

One summer Aunt Sanni and her two sons came to visit. Helvi and I slept in the barn loft and Sanni's two sons slept with her in our bed. Besides teaching us about how birds and bees made babies, she had a tube of toothpaste! She let us use it every day. It tasted good, not at all like salt or baking soda. The day they were leaving, I piled toothpaste the length of the brush and enjoyed the taste in my mouth. Aunt Sanni saw and smiled. "I'm leaving the toothpaste with you when we leave." I was surprised that she would leave something that expensive. For a second I wondered if she was generous because she was mama's sister or because she was really rich. With a mouthful of tasty toothbrush foam, I gurgled, "Thank you." Mama had said I should never forget to say that, so I thanked her right away while toothpaste dripped down my chin. Sanni wiped it off with her store-bought white handkerchief that was almost like a baby's bib. Mama sometimes called me her baby. I didn't like that, but it was nice of Aunt Sanni to baby me.

I ran barefoot that summer. It saved the wear on shoe leather; besides, Mama said sun was good for crops and kids. Tauno also ran barefoot. He had his head shaved because, he said, sun was healthful. Papa said the sun soaked into the leaves and roots of crops and made them grow. I believed it might make brains grow too, but my hair hung down to my shoulders like a rambling bush. I figured no amount of sun could reach my brain. Tauno had rosy cheeks. Maybe he got them from the sun soaking through his bare head. I wanted rosy cheeks too so I wanted to have my hair cut off. Why not? I had seen pictures of little boys with long curly hair like mine. Their mothers had not wanted to have it cut, or maybe they wanted their boys to be girls, just like I wanted to be a boy.

I asked Mama to cut off all my hair. She grumbled immediately. "Boys can get their heads shaved, but girls can't." But Mama couldn't stop me wanting a bald head. It would match my bare tanned legs and feet.

One summer Mama's other sister, who lived in Portland, came to spend a week with us. She had just divorced her husband, who was a tailor, and had no kids. Aunt Ida liked to sunbathe because a suntan was attractive. I heard Mama tell Papa she was a flirt and was looking for another man. I think this was the truth because Mama wouldn't lie about her sister any more than I would lie about Helvi, even though I didn't like her too well.

Papa had dug a ditch from the well and laid a pipe halfway to the house. There was a faucet, and Mama used a washboard to scrub our clothes. Ida filled Mama's big tub with water. It lay in the sun all morning. In the afternoon she invited me to keep her company while she sunbathed. She wanted me to get her a cupful of water when she got thirsty. That way she wouldn't have to get up. I didn't mind. While sunbathing, it was fun to learn a new song. She wasn't as good a singer as Mama, but that was OK, because I couldn't carry a tune either. Mama said I'd lost my voice after an adenoid and tonsil operation as a baby in an Idaho hospital. Papa was working there in a Burke Canyon mine some time after World War I started and we had moved there after I was born.

When Ida sang, I knew she was thinking of getting a new husband because of the song. It went like this:

Wherever you may linger,
Wherever you may go,
See to it that you have a mate.
Since you are already aging,
Your youth will soon be fading,
It won't return ever, ever again.

She would laugh and ask for water. I'd get it for her and then drink some myself. I was undressed also so I was getting a healthy tan like her. I wasn't looking for a man; I just wanted to be a boy and have a tanned body. The sun made streaks of blonde in my light brown hair, so I just knew my brain wouldn't get any sun and my cheeks didn't get rosy.

When Aunt Ida was ready to take her bath, she dipped some of the sun-warmed water into a washbasin for me. The water smelled wonderful: clean and sweet. It had been scented by the sun! I dragged the fragrant wet washrag over my face, then I swept it all over my body. I didn't have to scrub myself like Aunt Ida did; she had sweated a lot while just lying down on the grass doing nothing.

I felt clean and as fragrant as the lilac bush Papa had bought from the lilac lady who was like Luther Burbank, the potato king, Papa said. Her name was Hulda Klager. She lived in town. When our lilac bush was in bloom, it smelled like the sun-warmed water we had in the tub. Aunt Ida liked to smell good. She didn't go to the barn to help her sister, but I went as usual. That's the way sisters were, I figured. Helvi didn't come to help in the barn either. I did all the helping Mama needed there. I didn't want to wash the lilac sun smell off, but before going to bed, Mama insisted that I wash the bottoms of my feet. She didn't want the bed linen to get dirty. Mama saved the dirty wash water from my feet for the lilac bush. I figured the dirt my feet had picked up would feed the bush, as would the water sucked by its roots. Papa said we should give back to nature what we took out. That's what my bare feet did!

Having returned from the Idaho mines and established our farm while World War I was going on, Papa worked for a shipbuilding outfit across the Columbia River in Oregon. Mama was afraid we'd catch the flu that was going around. Like all the other Finnish women, Mama hung a stinky cube around our necks. It was supposed to kill any germs that dared to come near our bodies. When I lifted my blouse and got a whiff of that brown thing hanging inside my long underwear, I knew no germs would want to come near me. Those stinky cubes worked; none of us got the flu.

There was another treatment for avoiding colds. I didn't like that either. The other women on our hill did it also. A couple of drops of camphor oil were dripped on a cube of sugar and I had to eat it. It didn't work because I often had a snotty nose.

One evening I did my big job in the potty before going to bed. Mama saw some pinworms in it. I really got the works! Mama cut up a big onion and boiled it in a little water. When the onion was soft, she added some milk and let it come to a boil with the onion. Then I had to eat the mixture a spoonful at a time. It almost made me vomit, but when Mama told me I had to do something with that look in her eyes, I had to obey. I didn't have to like it, though. She made me eat it for two days. Finally, after studying the stuff in the pot, Mama said the pinworms were gone. That proved they couldn't stand the taste of boiled milk and onion any more than I could.

Years later when Papa came home for the weekend after a stint at the Mountain Timber Company as a tree faller, he said his back hurt. He lay down on his belly on the kitchen floor and asked me to take off my shoes and step on his back. He wanted me to place my feet on either side of his backbone and slowly move my feet up and down his spine. I was horrified. "Why can't Helvi do it?" Papa said Helvi was too big. He coaxed me to be a good girl; I was. I took off my shoes and did as I was told. "Move slowly up my back, one foot on the left side of my spine and the other on the right side." When my feet had gone halfway up his back, he directed, "Now go down the same way." I stepped backwards carefully. Papa groaned but muttered, "That feels good, Mirri." I

Before Modern Conveniences 37

liked to ease Papa's back pain. I wondered if a masseuse could work with her feet as well as her hands to get people feeling better. I guessed not; she would be too big like Helvi. Other farmers had back trouble, too, but I hadn't heard of any kid walking on their father's back. Maybe they didn't know it was helpful. Papa had studied at the Work People's College so he knew a lot of things the others didn't know. I was glad that I had helped Papa's back pain go away so he could go to work and earn money. We always needed money to pay the mortgage. The payments had to be made every single year.

    A number of men came over the years to rub Papa's and Mama's bodies. They were masseurs. They stayed overnight and ate all their meals with us. They charged one dollar a day for massaging both Papa and Mama in the morning and again in the evening. The house was almost as hot as a sauna during the massage. Mama and Papa would lie on the wooden bench in the kitchen with only a sheet over their whole body except the part that was being massaged.

In the evening when the masseur was working on Mama, Papa was busy greasing his leather boots. The grease was supposed to keep the rain from soaking into them. I didn't think it worked very well because Papa greased them so often. The masseur used lard on his hands when he massaged Papa and Mama. That way his hands could slide easily. There was a difference between grease and lard. Grease was tan, but lard was white. Grease was supposed to make the rain slide off Papa's boots and was used to lubricate wagon wheels; lard made the masseur's hands slide over the body and was used to make apple pies.

After we got our own sauna, a cupper woman came over to get rid of the rheumatism that both Mama and Papa had. Mama heated the sauna so there was a lot of hot water. The woman who did the cupping was highly respected in the Finnish community. After a person had bathed, the process began with a razor and a cone made from a cow's horn that had been hollowed out and cleaned. The horn had been cut at the tip and a narrow groove had been carved around the small end of the horn, which held the membrane, or fell, from a butchered animal's carcass. This was placed over the small end of the horn and string was wound around the groove to hold the membrane in a rigid position. It looked like a small curved drum.

The reason cupping was done in the sauna was that it was necessary for the blood to be drawn to the surface of the skin. The heat of the sauna did that. The cupper would place the horn over an area of the body where she had made a few tiny strokes with the razor; then she would suck on the membrane. After a few minutes, she would remove the cone so that blood would flow down the back or shoulders. The

Before Modern Conveniences 39

cupper then rinsed the blood away with warm water and did the same thing in another area.

I saw cupping done only once. That was enough. I thought it was terrible, but Mama and Papa agreed with everyone else on the hill that cupping brought out the "bad" blood. Mama said she felt better after having had a cupping treatment and Papa said that cupping was much better than having leeches suck out the bad blood, as kings and queens once did. I thought it might have been cheaper to get rid of bad blood the same way Mama got rid of my pinworms, but I didn't argue with Papa; he knew history and that was that. I had almost fainted when I saw the blood flowing from Mama's body. I wondered if I had been a boy, would I have been stronger and not felt faint.

I believed that looking at all that blood did my eyes no good. Several other kids at school also had red bumps on their eyelids, but I didn't know if they had the bumps looking at blood pouring from cuts made by cuppers. Maybe not; they weren't Finnish. Only Finns practiced that sort of old country cure. The school nurse said my eyelid bumps were sties. They didn't bother me, but they bothered Mama. Every evening she put a stinking warm wet rag on my eyelids. I had to hold it there for a long time, but Mama said it was only a few minutes. It didn't do any good; the sties were just as big and red the next day. Eventually they went away so Mama believed she had been a good doctor. I never thought of asking the other kids with sties if their mothers gave them the same treatment. Recess at schools was playtime, not talk time.

When the county nurse came to school to examine us kids, she told me that I had a cavity in my back tooth, a molar, she called it. She instructed me to tell my parents that I should have it taken care of before it got larger. I told Mama, who sympathetically asked me, "Mirri, does your tooth hurt?" Of course it didn't, or I would have complained. Then she said, "It isn't time yet to go to the dentist." A trip to the dentist cost money and we had to save for the mortgage payment.

After the county nurse had looked at my teeth, she asked me if I was constipated. I had never heard of the word. I thought that she was talking about going to the toilet, but I wasn't sure, so I asked her if she meant number one or number two. With a gentle smile on her face, she explained what constipation meant. I didn't want her to think that there was anything wrong with me so I answered, "Of course not." I felt guilty about that afterwards because sometimes Mama made me take a spoonful of castor oil so I could do number two.

I felt dumb not knowing the meaning of a long word like constipation so, out of curiosity, I asked several of my friends what they had answered. None of them knew what the word meant, but had answered "no" to the nurse. I told them what it meant and realized that I had taught them something. I had done the job of a teacher! Maybe I should become one. After I got through with school, I'd think seriously about being a teacher. It would be nice to tell kids what they ought to know. Mama said one learned a lot by working and asking questions. Maybe that's why Mama gave me advice all the time. Although she never went to school, Mama learned to read Finnish, write and count money by keeping both eyes and ears open and her mouth shut. She didn't have to keep her mouth shut anymore because she was teaching me, but I felt she should not scold me so much because I did the right thing—most of the time.

A year later many kids at school had the measles, but Helvi and I didn't tell Mama because we didn't want her to worry. When I got sick, had a fever, and didn't feel like eating, Mama knew something was wrong. Helvi felt well and had gone to school. Mama hitched the horse to the cart and took me to see Dr. Hoffman, the good-looking doctor in town. He had neither mustache nor beard like most of Papa's friends. The doctor knew everything and could make people well. The climb up the stairs was difficult. The doctor's nurse wore a clean white coat just like the doctor. She wrote our names on a pad on the desk and told us to sit down until Dr. Hoffman opened his office door to let us in.

The doctor asked a few questions that Mama did not fully understand so I told her what he had said, although I didn't feel like talking. Mama did not try to speak English because she knew she couldn't pronounce the words right, but she understood the doctor's slow explanation even before I translated it. I think she knew there was an epidemic of measles in the Northwest from reading about it in the Finnish women's paper published in Astoria.

The doctor put a tube stuck to a harness into his ears. On it was a pad that he placed on my chest. It didn't hurt. He listened to something. Mama told me afterwards that he had listened to my heart beating. He asked me to stick my tongue out. He held my wrist gently and watched his watch tick. All this time there was a thermometer in my mouth. When he took it out, he shook his head. I knew I had a fever before he said so. He wrote a prescription and told Mama to fill it with the druggist downstairs on the main floor.

Looking at me, Dr. Hoffman said that when I got home I must go to bed and keep the room dark. He told me to tell Mother that. I did, right then and there. The doctor was satisfied that I had translated what he had said. Even when I was sick, I wouldn't think of disobeying such an important man as the doctor in our town!

Leaving his office, Mama stood in front of the nurse with the white coat, opened her big black leather purse, put some money on the table and waited for the receipt. I knew the tube and the thermometer must have cost a lot of money. The stick he had used to keep my tongue down was just wood. There was a lot of wood in Woodland. I was sure that some of the money spent on me was what had been saved to pay the mortgage.

Going downstairs from the doctor's office was much easier than going up. Not many sick people climbed those stairs, Mama said. She told me that the doctor visited very sick people in their homes. That meant Mama didn't think I was too sick; I would get well, but that didn't make me feel any better.

Mama handed Dr. Hoffman's prescription to the druggist. He took it with one hand and with the other patted Mama quite low on the back. She pretended not to notice, but I saw that he also smiled at Mama. I couldn't imagine why; he had work to do. He turned quickly to the glass containers on the shelves that lined the wall. He put powder and liquid from several jars into a bottle and mixed the contents. While putting a cork on the bottle, he told me to take a teaspoonful every four hours, day and night. Mama laid money by the cash register. The druggist was honest because he gave some money back to her.

Although it was daytime, the trip home was a nightmare. The bottle with the brown liquid lay in Mama's purse. It wasn't doing me any good. After the horse had dragged us home, Mama unhitched it and took care of it before she helped me undress. Although she had told me many times I was a big girl, I lay on the bed and didn't do anything. Of course I was a big girl because I walked several miles to the school bus and I didn't get lost in the three-storied wooden school building in town, but today I didn't feel like walking or doing anything, not even getting undressed; I was that miserable.

When Mama came in from the stable, she gave me a spoonful of the brown medicine. It tasted good, not at all like the stuff she had given me for pinworms. She hung a blanket over each window. The room became dark. I felt drowsy and fell asleep. I slept off and on for days and days.

I remembered the beautiful horse I had carved...I wondered in whose stable it ate and whinnied and flicked flies from its back with its long slick black tail...I wondered if it had another horse now for a companion...I felt Mama's warm body next to me...It really was night since she never came to bed during the day. Papa was working at the timber company during the week so Mama was busy working except when she gave me the medicine. I didn't mind; it tasted good. I always fell asleep after swallowing a spoonful.

I heard Mama tell Helvi that the measles had broken out and that I would soon get well. The red splotches were all over my body. As I tossed and turned, I remembered that it was over two years since I had seen Wilho's behind when he had mooned me so I knew for sure that I was not going to have a baby. One had to be old and strong like Mama to have a baby. I felt relieved I wouldn't have to be bothered with looking after a baby and fell asleep. I woke up feeling much better.

Helvi didn't get the measles. I figured germs liked me better than her. I knew now what I wanted to be when I grew up: I wanted to be a nurse like the woman in Dr. Hoffman's office with the crisp white coat who had taken the money Mama had offered.

I heard Papa's cough before he walked into the house. He coughed a lot because his lungs were full of rock dust that he tried to get rid of. I slept in Papa and Mama's bed next to the wall. I heard Mama tell Papa how sick I had been. She said I had been a good patient and was well now. She said that on Sunday I would sleep with Helvi and the black blankets would be removed from the windows. Life would be normal again: Papa was home for the weekend.

My oatmeal breakfast tasted good the next morning. Helvi said she didn't mind my hanging around in the kitchen with her and she didn't even want me to help with the dishes. While she was cleaning up, I was busy turning the pages of her schoolbook so I wasn't happy to see Tauno show up. His greeting was simply, "Wow, you finally got well!" as if he had been waiting for me to be up and around. While chewing vigorously, he said he had something in his mouth that kept him from getting the measles.

Of course, I was curious. "You mean it's better than medicine?" He took a wad of something out of his mouth. "Look, it's pitch from a tree!" He pointed to the largest Douglas fir in our yard. He went to the tree and looked. There were several streaks of pitch flowing from it, but none met his approval; he said that the pitch wasn't the right texture on our tree. He walked away to play with Wilho, still chewing.

I was determined to be healthy like Tauno, who hadn't had measles. So, as soon as he left, I returned to the tree and fingered the pitch anxiously, but it stuck to my fingers. Another area of pitch produced a sticky substance—nothing that I could put into my mouth. The more I tugged and tore at the pitch, the stickier it became. My fingers were a mess.

Papa returned from the barn and saw my dilemma. After hearing my explanation, he laughed and escorted me to the bucket of water on the porch. He poured cold water into a nearby basin and told me to shove my fingers in it. The pitch solidified! I peeled it off.

Papa didn't scold me. He only said, "I don't think you'll ever do that again." Nor would I ever listen to what Tauno told me; he was just a boy.

4

U.S. Mail:
Our Connection to the Outside World

The delivery of United States mail was the most interesting event in our daily life. The mailman drove his horse and buggy from town, exiting up Green Mountain Road and then making the loop down the Butte Hill Road. He usually arrived in the middle of the afternoon. I liked getting the mail; I ran as fast as I could. As always, I was practicing to run in the Olympics.

One Saturday after I had delivered the mail at the usual coffee-time period of family relaxation, Mama glanced at the Finnish newspaper and shouted in joy. She grabbed Papa so suddenly that he found himself pulled up, turned around, and thumping his feet on the kitchen floor with Mama spinning him in circles. She was laughing and crying at the same time. "The war is over! The war is over!" Between the tears and laughter, came the words, "You won't be drafted!"

Papa snatched the newspaper from her hand and they both sat, heads together, and read the news. World War I had been over for a whole week, but they hadn't known! The only way anyone in our area received news was by reading the Finnish newspaper. Papa had been concerned how Mama could manage with us two kids if he were drafted. He was a U.S. citizen now, not like in Finland where all Finns were subjects of the Russian czar, who sent most of them to Siberia, to serve in his army there. As a U.S. citizen he was obligated to go when Uncle Sam called. Mama had assured Papa that she would manage somehow. She had a roof over her head, a cow and a few chickens. They had both worried that it would be a problem to get hay or supplies from town since she had no money, but all worries were over now.

    At the time Papa was working as a carpenter at a mill across the Columbia River and belonged to a union that published a magazine. It was not large so it was easy to hold in my hand as I pretended to read. Papa enjoyed my gibberish. I didn't really know what I was saying, but it sounded just like English.

Before Modern Conveniences   49

Going back and forth from the mail box, I felt like an Olympic runner. That was important, but today's mail had brought something that was better, a real prize: news that the war was over. Papa would not have to leave. He could stay home. I had brought him the news!

While getting the mail one summer, I found there were luscious strawberries growing beside the path. Naturally, I stopped to eat some. One day I thought I'd surprise Mama and Helvi with the sweet treat of a handful of bright red berries. They were partially crushed because I had held them too tight. While putting them into three small bowls and pouring thick cream over them, Mama asked where I had found them. She didn't know I had eaten more berries than I had picked for the three of us. I didn't say anything because I had worked to get them. Papa always said that work was necessary to get clothes and food. I liked the different taste of berries with thick cream on my tongue. So I ate, saying nothing.

When Papa came home, Mama told him about the strawberries I had found. Papa was interested. He asked me if there were many strawberry plants along the path. (I was the center of attention!) I told him that I had been eating some for several days and there were plenty of plants with little green berries that would ripen soon. Trying to show how observant I was, I said that some berries lay close to the ground and some were held aloft by a long stem. I was sure there were two different kinds of plants.

Papa listened carefully. After a moment, he said, "I have an idea. I'll contact the county agent and find out where I can get strawberry plants." Mama wondered what he had in mind. With a thoughtful look, Papa spoke as if dreaming. "I will raise strawberry plants and sell the berries to make money." Make money from strawberries?! Who would have thought of that? Papa did. If we liked to eat strawberries, surely other people would be willing to pay for them.

Papa took the Greyhound Bus to the county seat in Kalama to talk to the county agent. Several months later the mailman delivered a letter asking us to pick up the plants from the railroad depot. It was already fall, a good time to plant before the winter rains. The letter contained instructions about the way they should be planted and cared for. Papa asked me to read sentences he did not fully understand. Some words were too long for me so I looked them up in the little black English dictionary Aunt Ida had given us. (She had a lot of money so she could buy luxuries like a dictionary.) It was a big help because Papa seemed to understand, although it didn't make sense to me.

Helvi never helped in picking the right word in English. Whenever I asked her to help, she would reply haughtily, "I'm Mama's helper." Then she would add something I didn't understand: "You can't have your cake and eat it, too." She'd heard that silly statement somewhere, but I wasn't eating any cake, although I got my share. That was my right as a member of the family. After all, the milk I helped bring to the house was put into cakes. For no reason at all, Helvi blamed me for wanting to eat my share of the cake! Dictionaries made more sense than what she said. They explained words, not silly sayings.

Whenever we had cake, it was after mail was delivered at coffee time. I used to watch Mama and Helvi as they measured, sifted, mixed, beat and pampered the stuff in the bowl. Helvi's cakes turned out just as good as Mama's, but I thought they made too big a fuss doing all that work. I told them so. That's when Mama made the suggestion that I should make the next cake. I was excited, but Helvi was jealous that I might outdo her in her own work. I would show her how to cut short all that work!

The next day I took over Helvi's job to show her how to make cake baking easier. Since I knew what to put in, I got all the ingredients, one by one, from the pantry. It took only a few minutes to line them up and check I had everything. One after the other, I plopped the flour, sugar, butter, milk and flavoring into the bowl. I had a little difficulty cracking the eggshell with a knife, but I finally succeeded and was able to drop the yolk and white into the bowl without any bits of shell. (That was good since I had never done anything like it before.) I beat the mixture just like Mama and Helvi did and poured it into the prepared cake tin.

I could hardly wait to see what I had accomplished without beating the batter as much as Mama and Helvi did—as if cake baking were something special. Mama wanted to save as many eggs as possible to sell to the co-op so she could buy coffee, sugar and flour. They cost a lot of money, which was why we didn't have cake very often. We had to depend on money that Papa earned working away from home to make the mortgage payment, but milk and eggs provided the money for our everyday needs.

After the mail delivery, we were to have a party to celebrate my first attempt at baking a cake. The coffee table was already set as I opened the oven door. My dream cake was like a pancake! Helvi gasped and Mama sighed. Papa said, "Cut a chunk for me so I can taste it." Dutifully, I managed to hack off a chunk. Papa chewed and chewed. I held my breath to hear his verdict. With his mouth still full, he finally said, "After chewing it long enough, it tastes OK. It's got the right stuff in it." Swallowing, he managed to add, "Thanks, Mirri, but next time we have a cake, let Helvi make it." She smiled triumphantly. Dutifully, Mama joined Papa in eating the pancake. They dipped each piece into their coffee until it softened. Helvi and I dipped ours in a glassful of milk. Since we didn't have a pig at that time, the cake was eaten in a couple of days. The pancake wasn't wasted. For several days I was in no mood to run when I got the mail, but I did anyway.

Somewhat later Papa received a pamphlet from the Department of Agriculture in Pullman about growing strawberries. Papa had had me write a letter asking for information about the kind of soil in which strawberries should grow. It wasn't easy to do as neither of us knew how to describe our soil. I finally wrote a reply to Papa's satisfaction. Future success in our strawberry growing would depend on what directions we'd get. We all looked forward to a reply.

The mailman finally delivered an odd-sized package that I cautiously laid on the table. We didn't open it until Papa came to the house from working in the field. The package was neither a regular letter nor a real package. Anticipating advice about strawberries, I realized there was a lot going on in the world besides news that the mailman brought us six days a week. If all went well, we'd make money to pay the mortgage and not have to pay interest. Maybe I could order something I wanted from the catalog even if I didn't need it. That would be wonderful!

As soon as Papa entered the house, he opened the unusual package from Pullman. Along with the letter, there was a glass tube. What in the world was that for? Papa had me read the letter. I tried hard. I had to resort to my little black dictionary frequently to find words I did not understand. They needed a sample of the soil where the strawberry plants were. I thought it was odd that educated people would need a little bit of dirt from our hillside farm before giving us advice, but Papa said soil chemistry was important for the plants to get the right nourishment. He went out to get a sample. Having returned from the field, he placed the tube on a sheet of the previous day's newspaper on the table and shoved the dirt into the tube. The stuff Papa was shoving into the tube was dirt, the same kind Mama said I brought in on my shoes. Maybe when there was a lot of dirt together, it was called soil. Anyway, that's what educated people called it.

I didn't mind writing the address on the package, but I thought it wasn't necessary for me to write another letter. Papa insisted I did so. It was possible, he said, that they hadn't saved our original letter because sometimes letters were thrown into waste baskets. Or maybe they didn't believe in saving letters like we saved everything on the farm because Mama constantly muttered, "This might come in handy." I finally wrote the letter to Papa's satisfaction. I believed that he could have written the letter himself, but even Mama agreed that it was my duty to do as I was told.

Mama didn't like the way I sang. Even though I sang as loud as I could, she said I was out of tune. She thought of a trick to teach me to sing. One day, after she had picked up the mail, she held a letter aloft that was addressed to me. She said I was to listen carefully as she sang a line at a time and then sing with her, after which she would give me the letter. I didn't want to do it, but I wanted the letter so I sang the best I could. I liked to hear Mama's beautiful singing voice so I really tried to sing like her, but what came out of my mouth wasn't like hers. No matter how hard I tried, my words just came out louder, not better.

The envelope was postmarked from Astoria where Mama's sister Aunt Sanni lived, but the letter was from her son, Eino. It was written in Finnish. It wasn't difficult to read because one just had to pronounce every letter the way it was written. English was much harder. Eino's letter wasn't interesting because he just wrote about the Columbia River and the fish in it. He said a lot of the Finns had their own boats and went out on the Pacific Ocean to fish. He drew a couple of fish—as if I didn't know what fish were. I'd seen several that Papa's friend had snagged in his net in the Lewis River and sold to us.

Unlike many of her friends, Eino's mother didn't have to work in a fish cannery because her husband worked for the *Toveri*, a local Finnish newspaper there. Eino tried to make his letter interesting by drawing different kinds of boats and ships at the bottom of the letter. I didn't care for his drawings of boats with sails or paddles and ships with smokestacks. If he was trying to impress me, he didn't. It was not part of my world, but Mama said we all wrote about what we saw and heard around us. She reminded me many times that it was time I replied to his fishy letter, but I thought she just wanted me to get a letter in the mail so she could teach me to sing—even if I didn't carry a tune like she did.

Then came a letter from cousin Reino whose parents lived in central Washington. They were dry-land wheat farmers and had a lot more land than we did. Their farm was level, not hilly like ours. Mama made me sing to get his letter also. Cousin Reino was younger than I. Although I had never seen him, I wished I had because his life was interesting. He had a horse of his own and he rode bareback! His father did not work for a newspaper so his mother did not insist that he read and write Finnish. Even my Papa didn't say I had to learn Finnish. It was Mama who said all languages were important. You wrote Finnish words just as you pronounced them, except for the two letters that had dots over them. Those dots made brand new letters with a different sound. That's how simple it was, not at all like English. Even though Reino wrote in English, his spelling was not good, but that didn't matter. His letter was interesting.

Reino wrote that he had fallen off his "hors" because it ran underneath the "klowslyn" and the "hors nokkt" him off, but he wasn't "hert." He was just "shuk" up a bit. It was "gud" that the horse "stopt" and "terned" around to see what had "hapent" to him. That's how smart horses were. They didn't like to have kids fall off their backs. Horses liked to have boys ride on their backs; it was easier than plowing.

Reino drew a few horse heads at the bottom of his letter. Although they didn't look like real horses, I liked them better than Eino's boats and ships. I remembered the wonderful horse I had carved when I was a kid waiting for our very own home to be built. I thought that I could be a sculptor when I grew up. For now I decided to write a letter in English to Reino and hoped that it would help him become a better writer. Having written a reply to his letter, I felt like a teacher. I raised the metal flag on the side of the mailbox. That's how the mailman knew there was a letter for him to pick up before shoving the newspaper in. Each time I received a letter, Mama made me sing. No matter how hard I tried, she only sighed. Nevertheless, she always gave me the letter. It was better than not trying.

Shortly after women got the vote in Washington State, a neighbor woman down the hill trudged up to our home in the late afternoon. Mama suggested she should have picked up our mail. The woman was shocked. Nobody on God's green earth would take anything from anyone else's mailbox! The mailbox represented the government of the United States and nobody was allowed to open the flap except the mailman and the person whose mail was in it. Everyone had his name and mailbox number clearly written or printed on the outside of the box. It was no one else's business to open the mailbox. That was the unwritten law of the land. Everybody knew that, but Mama didn't. She just thought it would have been a neighborly thing to do because our mailbox was so far from the house. Mama agreed that laws had to obeyed whether they were written or unwritten and they went on with the business of organizing a women's club to talk about everything that they, as women, should know about elections.

Mama was a citizen, but she knew there was much for her to learn about the laws of the country. She had never taken a citizenship test like Papa. She got her citizenship simply by getting married to a naturalized citizen. That was the law at that time, yet she bossed me and I was a real citizen! That wasn't fair, but I didn't tell her that. It might hurt her feelings like she hurt my feelings. Laws made people respect each other even if they didn't have the same beliefs; I understood that.

The U.S. mail delivered Finns on our hill three different kinds of newspapers that had editorials and articles disagreeing with the other publications. The mailman was the carrier for our government, which supported freedom of ideas. The Finns sure practiced that freedom when they got together by quoting what they had read. Just to show how much respect Mama's friend had for the government, she never visited us

Before Modern Conveniences

again in the afternoon when the mail had arrived. She came over early in the morning instead.

One day Mama thought the chimney for our oil lamp, ordered from Montgomery Ward, might be delivered. As she wasn't sure if the package would fit into our mailbox, she asked me to wait for the mailman. I was pleased—anything to get away from Helvi, who was trying to get me interested in some embroidery she was doing. I thought the mailman had the world's best job, that is, a little better than being a teacher telling kids about other people in the world. His job was much easier than being a teacher. All he did was pull the reins and order, "Whoa," or whip the horse and utter, "Giddyap." He sat and sang as the two-wheeled cart came downhill.

The road was muddy from recent rain so, far away up the hill, the horse and buggy slowly lumbered down. The horse was stepping carefully in the middle of the road as the wheels were sunk deep in the ruts. It was pleasant work to be a U.S. mailman who just sat in his cart. His hardest job was to shove Finnish newspapers, letters, Montgomery Ward and Sears catalogs into mailboxes.

The catalogs had a lot of pictures of people. They did not look like any of our friends on the hill. I enjoyed looking at the old catalogs when I sat in the outhouse. I often stayed there longer than necessary to get out of chores. Every season we received new catalogs and the old ones were taken to the outside toilet, but it was nicer to call it a privy, which is short for private in English. Old Finnish newspapers were used to start the fire in the mornings and the leftover pages were cut into four equal pieces and taken to the privy. It was a long time since we'd used fern leaves.

The mailman's loud "Whoa, there!" broke into my rambling thoughts. He dropped the reins and handed me a newspaper as well as a long circular package. "Here's your doll," he said pleasantly. I was insulted. What did he think I was? Still a kid playing with dolls? As a matter of fact, I had never had a doll, just a teddy bear. Too upset to thank him, I indignantly grabbed the newspaper and package while informing him it was a chimney for our table lamp so we could read at night. I stomped my foot and turned around, thinking as I left that he wasn't such a smart man—even if he worked for the United States government.

My friend Riitta lived a mile down the road from our home. She was a year older than I, but we had the same interests. We liked to read something besides Finnish periodicals. Our parents read different newspapers so they had a lot of disagreements about everything going on in the outside world. They had their own ideas about religion, politics and unions. They got along, however, because they were Finns, shopping at the co-op and going to the hall.

At noon during school, Riitta and I often went to the drugstore and were given magazines in English. The druggist just tore the front page off and gave us the previous month's magazines that hadn't been sold. Inside were a number of coupons for free samples. All we had to do was write our name and address on the coupon and enclose it in an envelope with a two-cent postage stamp. After a while each of us got samples of perfumed soap that smelled like roses, better than the lilacs we had in our yard. (I didn't tell Papa that because he thought lilacs had the best fragrance in the world.) I once received a small sample of rouge in the mail, which tinted my suntanned face, but I still didn't look like a rose.

Getting those little packages in the mail was a special treat until Mama put a stop to it. Each time I sent in a coupon, the postage cost two cents, and the envelope had to be purchased. That was the end of our free gifts.

Both Riita and I colored our faces until the tiny container of rouge was used up. We rubbed the perfumed sample of soap on our necks until it was gone also. I thought our samples smelled like the expensive perfume in the drugstore where we got our free magazines. Unlike Mama, I was pleased the U.S. mail brought me that good smell for only two cents. It was fun pretending to be a stylish lady who had rosy cheeks and smelled good.

As I seldom now wrote to my two cousins and couldn't get free presents from magazines and I no longer smelled like a rose or had cheeks like one, going to the mailbox kept me in touch with the outside world via my thoughts of being an Olympic runner.

5

Visitors: Friends and Salesmen

Since farmwork kept everyone at home, it was a rare event when we had visitors. However, a broom placed diagonally across the kitchen door was a sign someone had come and gone in our absence. It was a disappointment for me when the visitors had not found us at home; consequently, wondering who had been at our door was a mystery that kept me guessing for days.

Sometimes the visitor had taken a drink from the water bucket that stood on the bench beside the door. The dipper from which we all drank was hung on a nail above the bucket. Papa held the handle a certain way so his mouth was always on one spot of the dipper. Mama drank from the rim a couple of inches away. Helvi and I were told to hold the handle in our left hand and thus drink from the other side. I think Helvi followed orders, but I was usually in too much of a hurry and too thirsty to shift the dipper to my left hand. Besides, I couldn't taste the difference between Mama and Papa's germs and I didn't see any germs on the dipper. Nobody watched how I handled the dipper. I just drank fast.

If the visitor had not replaced the dipper on the nail, I knew it must have been a kid. The dipper would then lie rim up, floating on the water, just as I left it in a hurry. Neighbor kids did not come over often so the telltale water dipper made me upset that I'd been away. Trying to comfort me, Mama would say, "People come and go for their pleasure or business, not yours." Even though we'd been out, I thought that it would have been nicer to have been home and perhaps had a playmate since Helvi seldom would play school with me because I wanted to be a teacher and tell her what to do.

There were lots of activities at the hall and sometimes speakers or actors would stay overnight at our place. They were from Kalama, Portland and even from as far away as Astoria. Having overnight visitors was a chance to celebrate. We were allowed to sit at the table with the grown-ups. Our table had a slick oilcloth that was easy to keep clean. Mama let Helvi pick the pattern for the oilcloth, but I wrote the order because Mama thought I had better handwriting. I liked that, but I would have liked to have chosen the pattern also. The colorful floral pattern Helvi picked was from Ward's, a huge mail order store in Portland, Oregon, from which we ordered everything that we couldn't get from our co-op.

It was a pleasure to sit at the table with out-of-town grown-ups and drink from a cupful of hot water mixed with a splash of milk and a sprinkle of sugar. Water and milk didn't cost anything. Coffee cost money and we needed money to buy coffee beans. It was my job to grind the beans into grains suitable for making coffee. I placed the coffee grinder between my legs as I sat. Mama poured the beans into the hopper at top. As I turned the wheel, the beans slid over the metal blades that ground them, dropping the grains into the drawer below. I liked the smell of fresh ground coffee. It was almost as good as drinking it.

Helvi said that grinding coffee was the only thing I could do well as I wasn't housebroken to do anything else. However, this inside job was much more pleasant than the smell Helvi had to put up with when she darned stockings. Sometimes she had to darn socks that hadn't been washed. They stank. Mama couldn't wash every week if she was busy doing something more important.

All work stopped when company came. That was a time for talk and coffee. I liked to listen to what other people said. Sometimes a man would pour coffee into his saucer, place a cube of sugar in his mouth and drink from the saucer. I thought that was old-fashioned, but I didn't say so. It wouldn't have been polite; he was company.

Tauno came over to visit us one day. He brought paper and a pencil with him because he was taking mail-order drawing lessons and wanted to show what he could do. Helvi was busy embroidering a handkerchief for Mama's birthday so she wasn't interested. Drawing was almost like sculpting, but not as realistic. I asked Tauno to draw a horse, but he wasn't interested. (Boys were supposed to be interested in horses so they could help their fathers. He just didn't know that.) He said he would draw our house. I watched his pencil sketch the shape of our house and the windows. Then he drew straight lines up and down with a few diagonals here and there.

"What in the world are those lines?" I asked.

Surprised, he answered, "That's what I see, the two-by-fours right here in front of my eyes," he replied as if I shouldn't have questioned an experienced artist. I told him angrily that pictures of houses should be from the outside, not the inside. "Besides," I added, "our house isn't finished yet. Papa will buy the lumber to finish the inside when he gets the money." I continued wistfully, "Our house will look like everyone else's then." Since he had been taking drawing lessons, I dropped the argument. Secretly I wanted him to draw something more important. I hesitated. Finally, bursting with curiosity, I asked, "Can you draw people?"

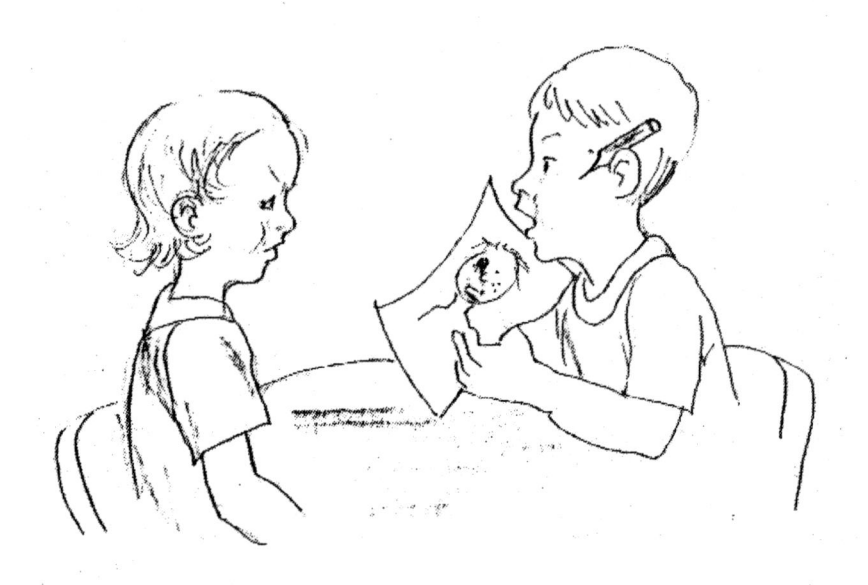

"I sure can. Would you like me to draw you?"

Would I like him to draw me? Of course! I often looked at myself in the dresser mirror in the bedroom so I knew what I looked like, but it would be great to carry a picture with me everywhere. While he drew, looking at me and then focusing on his pencilled lines, I asked if he would leave the drawing with me.

"Of course," he answered, "I don't want to keep a picture of you."

I was relieved. I knew boys put all kinds of junk into their pockets and I didn't want my face mixed up with that sort of stuff. I wanted to be a good subject for him so I sat still for several minutes. Then he ordered me to close my eyes so he could finish the picture. After a while he declared, "Time's up. Picture's finished," and shoved it across the oilcloth-covered table to me.

"What's that big blob on my eye?" I asked in wonder.

"That's your sty. Can't you see?"

I saw. I was hurt. "What's that on my chin?" I was furious.

He laughed and said that although it looked like a beard, it was the scab on the bruise that formed when I had fallen a few days previously.

The picture wasn't me; I was not a blob on an eye or chin! I didn't think Tauno knew how to draw and told him so. Although Mama had said that visitors were always welcome, he left in a huff and I was glad to see him go. I believed he was as angry as I was hurt. I saw him shove that picture into his hip pocket with all the other junk he had collected.

The Rawleigh traveling salesman was always welcomed by Mama. She bought vanilla extract every time he came over. That was the flavor she preferred over all others. Papa did also. Besides putting vanilla flavoring into the cakes she and Helvi made, she used it to flavor cardamom-bread puddings.

Mama also liked to buy colored thread and different sized sewing needles from the salesman. She used small needles for making us dresses from ones that her sister Ida, who lived in Portland, had given us. She was rich because she wore pretty silk blouses and skirts. When she got tired of them, she gave them to Mama.

Ida's husband was a tailor and made a lot of money just sitting and sewing, but Mama didn't make money from sewing. She just re-made Ida's clothes into dresses for us, which we wore when we went to the hall. So Helvi and I were well dressed with outfits from Aunt Ida's cast-off clothes. We grew so fast that Helvi couldn't wear her silk dress the following year. I wore hers, but nobody knew that because our dresses were identical.

The Rawleigh salesman came over shortly after I had broken a needle on our sewing machine. Mama had scolded me. Our Singer sewer was as particular as the separator! Mama said that my legs had not used the right rhythm so the needle broke. She didn't tell the salesman that because she couldn't speak English that well. I had broken the needle with the small eye and short stem for sewing silk. Mama liked medium-sized needles for sewing cotton and needles with large eyes for sewing patches on Papa's overalls. Consequently, she put in an order for needles of different sizes. Some of the needles were longer than others and had bigger holes for threading. Otherwise, they were the same. They were all sharp.

The salesman showed Mama a lot of objects she would have liked to order but could not afford. Nevertheless, Mama was interested as he unpacked a number of leather bags. Suddenly she picked out a round metal container and exclaimed, "This I buy!" You would have thought it was something special that had got her so excited, but it was for the cows!

Somebody had told Mama that Bag Balm was good for the udders of cows; it would keep them soft and in good condition. I didn't think cows cared what Mama bought, but I cared. I would have liked Mama to buy a bottle of maple extract. I had tasted cake flavored with maple at a neighbor's house and it was out of this world. Long ago we had had a maple tree on our farm, but it didn't give any syrup. Papa said maple syrup came from another kind of tree. Although our tree didn't give syrup, it was big and beautiful. Its branches stretched out, covering an old road that the mailman had used long, long before Papa had purchased our farm and where I had danced while Helvi picked dandelions. Mama didn't care what I wanted; she ordered vanilla extract only.

I looked forward to a certain salesman's visit as he made his rounds among the Finns. He had a poor reputation, and that meant a lot of things. He worked for a Midwestern woolen mill and only took orders for men's suits. Just a few farmers could afford to buy from him. They were the ones who didn't have a mortgage. They could splurge. He measured their bodies so the suit would fit properly. The farmers paid cash to the salesman and then waited for the suits to arrive. They waited…and waited. Over a year…over two years. The suits never arrived.

We heard through the grapevine that *Pullsitti Jäkki* (B.S. Jack) was making calls on our side of the hill where nobody had ordered a suit before. B.S. Jack happened to come over one afternoon when Papa and Mama were having coffee. He was better looking than any of the men on Butte Hill—even better looking than Dr. Hoffman. He was pleasant and spoke nicely, especially to Mama. She blushed. Papa sat silently sipping his coffee and started to scowl when Mama invited B.S. Jack to join them for coffee. He thanked her so nicely that I think Mama would have served him a meal if he had come during dinnertime. He told one joke after another that made Mama laugh. He often looked at Papa, trying to get him to smile in response.

Having finished his coffee, Papa smiled and said in a stern voice, "I might have ordered a wool suit from you if the men on the other hill had received their suits."

B.S. Jack acted surprised. With an expression that would have convinced anyone else, he said, "The suits were sent to them." As if hurt, he added, "They lied, spreading such gossip about me."

Papa uncrossed his legs, bent forward in anger and said that his friends didn't lie. Then he ordered B.S. Jack to leave immediately.

When the man drove away in his Ford, Mama joined Papa in laughter. Even I enjoyed the man's visit, but I felt sorry for him when Papa asked him to leave. His jokes were funny and I liked the way he talked so nicely to Mama. I wondered if he talked that way to all the other women in whose homes he had been.

He was the only visitor who was not welcomed in our home. As the salesman's car disappeared over the hill, I thought it would be nice to have a car, but we had to save money to pay the mortgage.

The most unusual event that ever happened on Butte Hill was the Koski roofing bee. The Koski home was at the top of our hill. Everybody came: men with tools, women carrying bundles of food, and we kids skipping around everyone. As soon as the men had drunk the coffee that was ready in the Koski kitchen, they departed to the barn. The sight of grown men stepping carefully on the barn rooftop and the sound of hammering amazed us kids. We hung around the Koski kitchen long enough to get bits and pieces of goodies that were unwrapped and then we girls congregated to explore the upstairs of the large family house.

Although we were high up in the second story, we didn't have any more of a view than from our one-story homes lower down the hill. A forest of trees of all kinds blocked the view. We didn't stay long. We were attracted to the main floor where an organ stood in the corner of the living room. Only the Koski boys knew how to play the organ, but they were at the barn or playing kick the can outside with the other boys. This was separation, different than at the hall.

Men were working on the barn roof, women in the kitchen, the boys playing rough games outside, and we girls were in the large living room enjoying the mystery of the organ. Although several of us touched the keys, we were unable to make any pleasant sounds. Without music, however, we danced together, chattered and giggled in the living room. At the same time we enjoyed the smell of food from the kitchen —and were not asked to work there! It was the most fun I ever had being with Helvi and so many other girls.

Tired of dancing, we looked for the boys, but they had gone to the barn. The Koski lilac bushes were larger than ours, which meant they had purchased them much earlier. They were in bloom and I admired their dark lavender color, much prettier than our bush that had light lavender blooms. Walking around the house, we saw the half-basement, containing a barrel in which the Koskis churned butter and made buttermilk for the family. Further down the path near a spring was their sauna with a separate dressing room. They were established farmers! Some day, I knew, we'd have a sauna, but we'd never need a barrel to make butter. Our family was not large.

Hearing a gong from the house, we ran back through the kitchen door. Overhead guns hung on nails on the wall. There was one for each of the five boys. Papa said they helped supply the family with a variety of fresh meat from the forest. The food spread on the long table today, however, was not from the forest. It had been brought by the women further down the Butte Hill road. We girls joined the barn-roofing-bee refreshment party without having worked!

From early fall through late spring every year our family placed a green "Welcome" mat in front of our porch. It was made from Douglas fir boughs. The butts were shoved beneath the softer fir branches. It looked like a large green fan welcoming the few people who had the time to visit.

Before entering the house, everybody wiped the mud off their shoes or boots on it. Mama liked that. I liked the visitors better.

The personal welcome at the barn-roofing bee was the smile of every single Butte Hiller who attended. It was fresher and livelier than the lonely Douglas fir fan that lay in front of our home.

6

Work: Part of Daily Living

Mama's main topic of conversation—work—began as Papa and his helper laid the foundations of our new home. After they had built the outhouse, Mama walked around the form of the house, looked puzzled and then asked Papa, "Where will the pantry and clothes closet be?" Papa, with his usual patience, answered that money was scarce for building unnecessary additions. A moment later he said, "It'll be cheaper to hang clothes on nails in the bedroom for the time being." As if to satisfy Mama, he added, "We'll build shelves for supplies on the kitchen wall."

Mama faced Papa and his friend with hands on hips and her head thrown back. "I lived in a one-room hovel in Finland as a sharecropper's daughter." She drew a deep breath and continued, "We didn't even have nails for clothes; we wore the only clothes we had." She took a step or two towards Papa and continued, "The only place we put food was in a pot or basket on the floor. Sometimes we had nothing to put in there."

While carving that horse on the ridge near the construction, I saw that Papa was changing the foundations. It was an extra area halfway between what was to be the kitchen and the bedroom. Mama had got her way: she would have a pantry and a clothes closet.

As soon as we moved into the house, Mama told us what we were to do. "A house can be a home only if everyone takes part in the work that needs to be done." She continued in a halting manner, "Helvi and Miriami will do most of the chores in the house." She gave a faint smile. "It's easy work, but very important for our health. Sharing chores makes a family." Mama added that everyone must pitch in because the mortgage had to be paid. Then we would be homeowners! Mama had never lived in a home of her own like Papa had in the old country. Until now Papa and Mama had always lived in rented houses or apartments. Life would be different now. All we had to do was to work toward our common goal: a home of our own!

After we moved into our new house, Helvi and I cleaned the table after each meal, washed and wiped the dishes and put them where they were supposed to be placed in the pantry. The dishpan stood on the corner of the wood stove and the pan with the rinse water was near the firebox. That water got hot very quickly so I picked up the glasses and plates and wiped the dishes as fast as possible to avoid getting my fingers scorched. I didn't like the job.

One day I danced while flinging the dish towel up, down and sidewards as I kept in tune with the melody ringing in my ears. It was a song that Mama always sang even while working. While absorbed in my fantasy, waving the dishtowel, the plate suddenly flew out of my hand. It crashed on the floor. I was shocked. Plates cost money! "You are absolutely crazy," I heard from Helvi as she saw the mess on the floor. Ordering me about as if she were Mama, she said, "Better sweep that up before Mama gets back from milking!"

I was terrified as to what Mama would say. I had been lost in a dream world but that was no reason to let go of the plate. I felt guilty. Mama came into the house before I had swept all the broken pieces from the floor. Helvi told her right away what I had done. Mama looked at the bits and pieces left on the floor. Finally, after surveying the scene, she said in a matter of fact tone, "I think it's time for you, Miriami, to help me in the barn." Turning to Helvi, she added, "I am sure you can handle the entire dishwashing much better alone than with your sister."

I was surprised that I wasn't being punished. I was also relieved at Mama's proposal as I liked the idea of going to the barn. Helvi was getting to be too bossy. Her way of bossing me was worse than Mama's, maybe because I was her sister. If I had been her brother, I don't think she'd have bossed me like she did.

Mama didn't waste time scolding me. She swept the rest of the broken china into the dustpan and went to the woodshed. She dumped the pieces on a block of wood and chopped them into tiny fragments with the blunt end of the hatchet, "to feed the chickens," she said. Not knowing any better, chickens would peck up the fragments as if they were grit to help grind the grain in their gizzards.

Whenever we had boiled or fried eggs, Mama dried the shells, then crushed them into tiny fragments to feed the chickens. She said the calcium in the shells made new eggshells stronger. Nobody wasted anything in the old country and Mama wasn't going to waste anything here. Nature, she claimed, supplied us with a lot of things that could be used over and over again, "if we were wise enough."

The chickens roosted at night. They wrapped their claws around poles in our chicken lean-to. They stuck their heads under their wings and went to sleep. When a hen wasn't laying eggs, Mama would chop its head off, then soaked the hen in hot water so the feathers could be plucked out more easily. She saved feathers for years and years in an old flour sack. When the sack was full, she sewed the open end shut and washed the feathers in boiling water. Even if mama did this when the sun was out, it took several days for the feathers to dry in the sack. She didn't take them out because a gust of wind might blow the feathers all over the yard. In order that the feathers would dry faster, she often adjusted the feathers in the sack; it looked as if she were molding bread dough.

When the feathers were dry, she enclosed them in another clean flour sack and sewed the open end shut by hand. I didn't think her home-made pillow was as good as the one ordered from the mail order company. The backbones of the larger feathers poked through the thin cotton covering of the homemade pillow. Mama said she should have used

Before Modern Conveniences

only the pin feathers because they were soft. When she talked about pin feathers, she was not referring to the really sharp staight or safety pins that we used when we were too much in a hurry to sew properly.

Chickens produced something else for us. Mama didn't give the bones to the dog because she had heard chicken bones sometimes got stuck in a dog's throat and the dog had to be shot. If you shoot a dog you've been feeding for years and years, it's wasting money. Dogs guard the farm. Mama crushed the chicken bones also in the woodshed to feed to hens and roosters. They didn't know what they were guzzling and I didn't know how to tell them about the possible danger of using their own bones to crush grain in the gizzard.

Mama also chopped off the wings of the chicken she had killed and then boiled the wings in hot water. She later washed and dried them and they became dusters in our house. They were easy to hold and did a good job. Mama used those chicken wings to wipe off the flour from the wooden board on which she rolled and tossed bread dough. Helvi used the chicken wings to wipe crumbs off the oilcloth on the table. She used a wet dishcloth when I spilled something. I did that often. I never intended to make work for her, but she didn't think it was an accident.

I liked helping mama in the barn. When I first went there, she told me to hold the cow's tail during the fly season. Sometimes I had to hold it with all my strength when the cow tried to flick the flies from her flanks. A tail is like a muscle, somewhat like a baseball bat and just as hard to hold. Once when looking at the kittens waiting for milk, I forgot and loosened my grip on the cow's tail. That's when the cow succeeded in slapping mama's face. The sudden blow on mama's cheek brought only a reminder for me to pay attention to my job. (Mama said I had a job! I liked that!) Even if she was hit in the face, she kept on milking until there was no more milk in the teats. She poured milk into the little pan and let me hand it to the cats. I liked watching the cats lap it up.

Cows are said to "get fresh" when they have a baby. It's called a calf. I taught the calves to drink from a bucket by sticking two fingers into its mouth and shoving the head partway into warm milk. I was careful not to shove its nose into the milk because they have to breathe even when drinking. It took only three or four days for a calf to drink milk from a bucket without having my fingers in its mouth. Although people are smarter than calves, babies don't learn in a few days to drink milk even from a little cup.

After a couple of months, papa would say the calf was the right size for butchering. Our calf had been fed whole milk so papa would get top price for it. He knew I was curious about everything he did so he told me to stay away from the woodshed when he butchered the calf. Despite that, I peeked around the corner as he banged the calf on the head to stun it and then pierced its throat with a knife. I thought that was awful. I felt sorry for the calf. I was angry at papa. I would never do anything like that. I ran back into the house. Helvi didn't sympathize with me. She said it was my own fault if I was upset. I had not obeyed papa. I didn't dare tell mama because she would take sides with papa. Papa didn't want me to see him do something so terrible as killing an innocent calf. Mama didn't like to see me do anything unless it was what she wanted. That's a lot of difference in the way they bossed me.

One Christmas Helvi insisted that I do my share in making a gift for Mama and Papa. She pestered me so much that I finally agreed. She had ordered a set of pillowcases from a catalog. "HIS" was stamped on one pillowcase and "HERS" on the other. Helvi taught me how to cross-stitch the HIS and HERS, and she chose the color I was to use. She kept busy crocheting a two-inch wide strip that she would later sew onto the open end of the pillowcases. Helvi told me to sew evenly. I did my best. She thought I did a good job. It was nice of her to say so.

We hid the gift until the 25th. That was not easy to do because Mama watched everything that was going on, but we managed. We saw what she was going to give us: the usual pair of knitted mittens. Since my mittens shrunk when I played in wet snow, they were always too small for me the following year. I would see Mama unravel the old mittens and use the wool over and over again, but my fingers didn't care. The mittens kept my hands warm until I played in the snow. Since it didn't snow every winter, Mama would knit instead a pair of woolen stockings. They were uncomfortable in school but they kept my legs warm on the long walk to and from the school bus. Our stockings never had holes in them. We had to keep them darned—Mama saw to that.

Mama looked puzzled when we gave her the pillowcases at Christmas, but she thanked us, just like she had taught us to thank anyone who gave us something. The next morning Helvi and I were shocked to see that Mama had put the HER pillowcase on Papa's pillow and the HIS under hers. When we told her that was wrong, she asked, "What's the difference between 'his' and 'hers'?" Since I always spoke up first, Helvi let me explain. That's when I realized the Finnish language did not have words for his and hers. No wonder Mama did not understand! The Finns use the same pronoun, *hän*, for referring to the person they were last talking about so there was no confusion. Mama had had her first lesson in English from her "baby" as she sometimes called me, and Helvi and I had learned something about the language we used at home that we hadn't noticed before. It was a real gift, in a way, for all of us and it made me feel like a teacher. But I knew teachers read a lot of books and did not spend time cross-stitching Christmas presents, as I did.

One Christmas Papa carried a Douglas fir tree into the house. He set it up in the middle of the kitchen floor. Helvi and I decorated it with paper chains made from a wallpaper catalog. We cut the pages into strips and pasted them into circles. Mama showed us how to make paste out of flour and water. Helvi said I made a mess out of my chain, but it was hung on the tree just like hers. The fir needles covered all the exposed white flour paste.

Papa had bought cranberries from the co-op because he wanted to support some friends of his who grew them in Grayland, a town on the Pacific coast. We threaded a large sewing needle and shoved it through one cranberry after another, creating a long red chain. Helvi and I draped it on the tree. The contrast of colors was nice. We had to detour around the tree to get from the stove to the kitchen table. Christmas seemed right in our midst! Mama baked a cake for dessert and sang a holiday song. We liked that.

While helping Helvi clean up after the holiday, I realized none of our decorations really belonged in the house. The tree belonged on a nearby hill and the cranberries in a bog on the coast. We should have had the money to order wallpaper from the catalog instead of making chains out of it. I was glad I hadn't thought of this earlier for I enjoyed our holiday, even though our kitchen was crowded.

If a farmer wanted to increase the size of his herd of cows, the services of a bull are needed. We didn't have one. Whenever a cow was in heat, it needed to be bred. A farmer who lived down the hill had a bull but he charged a whole dollar. Mama insisted that I take a switch and follow the cow as she led it down the road. I did not mind doing that because I didn't have to stay in the house with Helvi. The cow followed Mama well, so I didn't have to whip her. She had made the trip a year ago.

The farmer brought the bull out of the pen and stood smoking his pipe while the bull did his job just like a rooster does to a chicken only not as quickly. I thought having a bull was an easy way to make money and we should have one. Mama said some people, she heard, would go a second or a third time to have another cow serviced but claim that it was the same one. All for the same dollar! They lied, of course, when they said, "It didn't take last time." Since some farmers have cows that look alike, it was hard for an outsider to know one from the other. "Not all Finns are honest," mama remarked, but I thought having a bull of our own would save a dollar. I could think of a lot of things I would like to buy with that much money. They were my wants. Mama said we had to take care of our needs first before we could get our wants satisfied. But I still wanted this and that. The return trip was different. I had to switch the cow often. Although we had plenty of feed for her, she didn't want to go back home to our new barn. I wondered why.

There was a time when the calf grew so big in the cow's belly that she slowly went dry. That was the time mama thought I should learn to milk. The very first time that I sat underneath the cow on the wobbly three-legged stool, I did everything I was supposed to do. I washed the cow's udder with warm water and put some salve on my thumb and forefinger and proceeded to draw milk. It looked nice to see the white stream hit the bottom of the milk bucket with a clanking sound. I was pleased. All went fine until the cow slowly lifted her leg and then suddenly shoved her hoof into the bucket! I felt like crying but I was already going to school so I wasn't a baby anymore even if mama sometimes still called me her "baby."

Mama turned her head slightly as she continued milking and told me to shove my head into the cow's hip joint so she wouldn't be able to raise her leg again. She advised, "Look where I hold my head." As if to assure me, she repeated, "The cow can't raise its leg." Her bucket was three-fourths full. The milk looked like beat-up egg whites. That's how foamy it was, a sign of an expert milker. I shoved my head just like mama did. There wasn't much milk left in the cow's udder. So I picked up the bucket and clutched the three-legged stool as I rose from my first experience of milking. Mama ordered me to pour the milk for the cats. Not knowing the cow's hoof had been it, the cats just lapped up the milk as usual. I was told to carry the bucket to the milk house and wash it. I was glad the cow was almost dry so only a little milk was wasted.

The hardest job in the barn was to shovel manure from the stalls. The foot-wide trough stretched from one end of the barn next to the door where the cows entered to the other end, the calf pen. Cows are messy animals even if their milk is clean and wholesome. Cows don't always drop their "pancakes" in the trough. Sometimes they move their bodies sideways and let go. Then they lie down on it; maybe they like its soft warmth! After it had dried on their flanks, it was my job to brush it off. Some cows are messier than others. Mama said that's the way it is with people also. But cleanliness is important even in the barn.

When we had five cows, papa and mama decided we should have a pig. That meant papa had to order a separator from a mail order catalog. It wouldn't make sense to feed whole milk to pigs so milk had to be separated. Pigs could thrive on skim milk and leftovers from the house.

The separator was a machine that funneled cream away from the milk. The cream poured out of a smaller spout than the skim milk. Mama sold the cream to a collection depot in town which, in turn, sold it elsewhere to make butter. The handle of the separator had to be turned a certain way or the machine wouldn't work right. Mama showed me how it was done. She called it rhythm, the same speed turning the handle whether it was away from me or towards me. It wasn't easy but I liked doing it. It was exercise so I thought it would make me strong like a boy.

While I turned the handle of the separator, mama busied herself adjusting the containers underneath the spouts and refilling the big tank on top with milk. This was not a chore; it was an important JOB that I was doing. Jobs help make money to pay the mortgage. I had to keep my mind on what I was doing or the speed of the separator changed and I'd hear mama's warning voice which meant the separator wouldn't be able to do a good job separating cream from skim milk.

Washing the separator disks was very important. They had to be washed very well and rinsed in hot water. If it wasn't done properly, the cream would go sour and we wouldn't be able to sell it. Once when the cream did go sour, Mama used it to make sour cream butter for our own use. I couldn't tell the difference in the taste. Mama could. Her sense of taste was as sharp as her tongue. She was particular about washing the separator disks because there were so many thin round plates that whirled around, throwing the cream aside into the little spout. Mama said over and over again that each plate had to be washed clean, clean, clean. It rung in my ears. I had to do my job well to help make money to pay the mortgage.

The root cellar, located halfway between the barn and the house, was always cooler than the outside air during the summer. In winter it was warmer than the outside air. Papa said the reason we had a root cellar was to store food. Our cellar had an attic above it where we kept a supply of apples during the winter. If there was a danger of frost, we would cover the apples with hay and an old moth-eaten blanket.

When the soil was not yet ready for planting potatoes in the spring, it was my job to sit in the root cellar and rub off the sprouts of the potatoes. With the door slightly open, I would sit on a stool in the semi-darkness, rub the long sprouts off each potato one by one and think of all kinds of things I would do when I grew up. When the de-sprouting was done, I still hadn't decided what I would do. Papa said I had plenty of time to decide. He knew best because once he had been a boy and now he was a man.

. During the right time in the spring when the ground was in proper condition to plant potatoes, Papa plowed furrows in the field. Mama and Papa cut a large potato into several parts so we'd get more plants started. At least two or three eyes were left on each chunk. The eyes weren't really eyes; they were the buds from which sprouts grew and made new plants.

    Mama and I dropped a chunk of potato just about a foot apart into each furrow, . It was boring to walk astride the furrow and drop the chunks into the soil. When my bucket was nearly empty, Mama took over. She told me to run to the root cellar to get more chunks for planting. I ran like an Olympian!

    There was a time in the fall when the potato plants were past their prime, like the wrinkled faces of old men and women. That's when even Helvi had to join in picking the potatoes. Papa plowed deep and the potatoes were brought to the surface, but some of them just liked to snuggle in the soil. To get at them, we used a hoe to dig them up. Regardless of how careful we were, sometimes the tines injured a potato. When our buckets were full, we'd carry them to the root cellar and sort them into three bins: one for large potatoes, one for smaller potatoes and one for the bruised ones, which Mama handled with care, like a nurse.

    Sometimes the holes our hoes made were deep and full of dirt. We never ate any of the dirt that I know of—Mama made sure of that. Dirt was only good for crops to grow in, not for our tummies. Mama baked the big potatoes. She boiled the medium-sized and little ones with their skins on. The bruised ones were peeled, cut, boiled and served as mashed potatoes. It took more work than baking or boiling potatoes, but I liked mashed potatoes the best. I was always hungry and mashed potatoes didn't take as much chewing so they filled my tummy faster. Since Helvi did the work in the kitchen, mashed potatoes were not her favorite food.

Before Modern Conveniences

All the potato peelings were put into a bucket for the pig. We called it the slop bucket. Helvi said my stomach was a slop bucket because I devoured anything within reach. Mama said I should ask to have food handed to me. Helvi was fat and didn't eat much, while I was skinny and ate a lot—before it was thrown into the slop bucket.

All the food we ate was prepared on our big, black, cast-iron stove. It burned up a lot of wood and made ash, which dropped down into a container below the firebox. My job was to carry the ash and spread it underneath the fruit trees. Mama scolded me the first time I did the job because I dumped all the ash underneath my favorite plum tree. I wanted it to get more "food" than the other trees. It didn't work that way. The next day the wind changed direction and blew the ash away from the entire orchard! I didn't always have to carry the ash box because Mama did it sometimes when there was no fire in the firebox and we were at school. Unless she was baking, Mama let the fire go out when she was working outdoors with Papa. That saved wood for the winter.

I had a dog by the name of Shepy. It was short for Shepherd, its breed. I trained it to carry a chunk of wood. When I went to the woodshed, I called, "Shepyyyyyy, come here!"

He'd come running. He liked attention as much as I did. He'd wag his tail and drool until I gave him a chunk of firewood to put in his mouth. He'd trot with me to the kitchen door and then drop the wood. I'd say, "Good boy." After getting rid of my armful of wood in the wood box that stood next to the kitchen stove, I'd return and pat Shepy. He'd wag his tail like a windmill. We'd make the trip back and forth until the wood box was full. After having a bite to eat on returning from school, filling the wood box was the first job Shepy and I did, always together, rain or shine.

Shepy never greeted Helvi. She didn't like dogs jumping around her. She didn't want her school clothes to get dirty. That was dumb of her because Shepy stopped jumping the moment I asked him to stop. He was a good boy; he obeyed me. Helvi did not care for any of our animals—dog, cats, cows or horses—although they were all workers on our farm. Our dog kept prowling wild animals away from the farm, the cats killed mice, and everyone knew how necessary cows and horses were.

Helvi wasn't a farm girl at heart. When I heard someone ask her how many cows we had, she said she didn't know. She just didn't have an inkling about our animal kingdom. (I heard a teacher use that word. That didn't make sense to me. We didn't have kings in this country, so how could our animals live in a kingdom?) I didn't understand everything I heard from a teacher but I liked to use this term.

After I found strawberries on the pathway to the mailbox, Papa ordered some plants.

When a big carton of strawberry plants from the county agricultural agent was delivered at the train depot, Papa had the field ready for planting. Mama and he did the planting when we were at school. Every plant looked as healthy as plants were supposed to look, Papa said, and he was happy with the small green marbles that grew larger daily and changed color. As soon as the berries ripened, Helvi and I picked the big Marshall berries. Papa told us to be sure to keep the hulls on the berries and pick only the ripe ones. They were dark red and sweet. Papa sat underneath the biggest fir tree in our yard and sorted the berries into a hallock. He put the biggest berries on top so the display looked nice. There were 24 hallocks in a crate. When he sold the berries to the co-op, he paid each of us one cent for each hallock we had picked.

I earned twenty-five cents the first day. I felt sorry for Helvi. She didn't earn as much as I because she was so slow. Even though Mama always advised me to go slow, it really paid to work fast! I felt rich. Maybe Mama and Papa felt that way too. When Papa came home from town, Mama put the coffee pot on to celebrate. Money from strawberry sales was put aside to pay the mortgage.

It was nice to earn money every single day when the berries were ripe. The weather was perfect so berries ripened every day. Mama said I could do whatever I wanted with the money I earned, provided my decision was okayed by her. I craved to have store-bought clothes from Sears or Ward's. Then Mama wouldn't have to make my dresses anymore. I wanted to earn money to clothe myself. Although girls weren't allowed to handle horses, we were just as good, if not better, than boys at picking strawberries.

Since I was paid for picking strawberries, I worked hard and fast. I would pick berries while bending. When my back got sore, I'd pick berries with one knee on the ground. Then, for a change, I'd pick with the other knee on the ground, balancing my body as my fingers plucked the berries. After a while, I picked while crawling on both knees. The knees of my overalls got dirty, but I didn't care as long as I had filled the hallocks. Papa made a carrier that held six of them. The carrier had a handle so it was easy to move as I crawled my way up the row. Helvi did not crawl on her knees like I did so her back was sore at the end of the day. That's why she didn't earn as much as I did. She was glad when the strawberry season was over. I wasn't. I liked the money.

Mama washed my overalls. They were worn out at the knees. She suggested that if I mended the knees, I wouldn't have to buy another pair. Mend my overall knees? Why not? I could save money for a dress. I let Mama know that I would go for it. "It isn't at all like darning the holes in your stockings," Mama warned in her matter-of-fact voice. Picking strawberries while crawling on my knees had worn holes at both knees. Helvi's overall knees weren't worn out at all. If I patched my overalls, we both could buy something we wanted!

Mending overall knees turned out to be a difficult job. Mama got a pair of Papa's old clean overalls that she had stacked away. She showed me how big a patch I was to cut from them. First I had to turn my overall leg inside out and sew the patch over the hole by hand. Then I had to turn the overall leg right side out. I had to turn under the edges of the hole and sew along the edge to attach the patch to Papa's old overalls. In an hour it was done. It looked OK.

Before Modern Conveniences

Mama said that was only half the job. "You must now use the sewing machine over everything you have sewn by hand." I objected. I didn't like using the sewing machine. That was Helvi's job. Sounding like an army general, Mama exclaimed that the holes in my overall knees were a result of my work, not Helvi's. "Sewing by hand won't last with the hard work you do." That did it! I did harder work than Helvi! I was just as capable outdoors as Helvi was indoors so I tackled the sewing machine to get what I wanted: money to buy a dress!

Again I heard the words, "Take your time, don't hurry." Then came my real challenge to follow orders. "If you hurry and break the needle, I will charge you five cents for the cost of the needle." Sewing was much more difficult than milking cows, but I did it! It took me all day to sew the patches on my overalls. And I didn't break a needle so I didn't need to buy a new pair of overalls. "Patches are honorable," Mama said. She let me know that it was OK to be naked in the sauna taking a bath, but not to show off even bare knees elsewhere.

Milking cows had become routine. I could milk so well that foam would form on top of the milk in the bucket like it did on Mama's. I felt like a baroness in the barn and wanted to show my authority by making a change in the usual order of the cows entering the barn.

I didn't like the idea that Rose, the lead cow, always came in first and went to her stall by the door. The other cows ambled into the barn after her, one by one, and went to their places. My favorite, all-white cow was different form the others. She was forced by the other cows to come into the barn last. One day I decided I'd make a change to that sort of discrimination. Holding a whip in my hand, I didn't allow Rose to come in first. She got confused and turned around, then tried a second time, but I wouldn't let her enter. I whipped and yelled at the cows, who became confused by the change. Finally, I coaxed Nellie, the white cow, to come in first. Success! No more discrimination in our herd!

Rose, who had been watching my whip, came in next and was followed by all the others. Bedlam! They shook their heads and horns at Nellie, who backed away from Rose's stall while still holding a mouthful of hay. Rose entered her own stall. The other cows swung their tails, heads and horns at Nellie, who finally scampered to her usual far-away stall next to the calf pen.

Discrimination of all kinds takes place everywhere, Papa said, but I didn't know it was also the natural order with animals. Papa said changing the customs and thoughts of people was just as difficult as changing the pecking order in the barn. Nellie's place was set by the herd, not me.

I still felt sorry for the treatment that Nellie had to put up with. While I brushed all the cows every day, I brushed Nellie longer. I also gave her an extra pat on the rump. That way I practiced my own form of discrimination.

7

The Games We Played

Sometime after having moved into our new home, Tauno's mother invited my parents to come for afternoon coffee. That meant both Helvi and I were to go there with our parents. I wanted to roam around our new home. I complained about going. Knowing that I was always hungry, Mama influenced me by saying that Tauno's mother was going to serve apple pie. We didn't even have an apple tree and I hadn't ever tasted an apple pie. It must be something special! I quit fussing and ran ahead of everyone to get there.

While the old folks were sitting around the table talking and waiting for the coffee to be ready, Tauno suggested we go outside to play "Andy, Over!" It was a game where you threw a ball over the roof at the same time as shouting so loudly that Andy, on the other side of the house, could hear and catch the ball. He was then supposed to throw the ball back. There was nobody on the other side of the house but an old maple tree, and it could only stand and wave its branches. Tauno said we were supposed to pretend. I understood that; I did it often.

"Do you have a ball?" Helvi asked anxiously, as she had seen one of the kids at school with a ball. She had even been given the privilege of throwing it once. "Heck, no," Tauno replied with the voice of authority. He added, "We'll just use these clay lumps. They're as hard as rock so they'll do OK."

Tauno picked up a large clump and threw it over the roof. Helvi found a suitable one, twisted her body, flung her arm high in the air and forward. To our pleasure, she succeeded in throwing it over the roof. Tauno shouted. "Wow!" He was surprised that a girl could throw that well. I was going to show that I could do even better. I didn't hesitate for a moment. I picked up the biggest and hardest clump of clay nearby and threw it with all my might. It crashed through the kitchen window and landed on the uncut apple pie on the windowsill! I was shocked.

A roar rose from the folks inside. They called us to come inside. Helvi grabbed my hand. (Did she think I was going to run away?) Although I was upset that the clay clump hadn't flown over the roof, I marched along with Helvi, feeling like a criminal.

"You've done it again," Helvi sputtered. When I hesitated at the door, she pushed me into the room. Standing firmly behind me to expose the culprit, she shouted, "It was Miriami who broke the window!" Tauno loudly declared that his ball had flown over the roof. That wasn't the real truth; it was just a pretend ball. We had all played that game. Why was I alone going to be punished just because my aim was so low?

Flustered, I managed to sputter, "But I just tried to throw the hunk of clay over the roof." I added, "I missed. I'm sorry."

Instead of scolding me, Mama turned to Helvi. "You are older and should have had the sense not to let Miriami throw anything." But Mama should not have scolded Helvi; she couldn't have stopped me because she wasn't my mama. Nobody could have stopped me from playing the game with Andy who wasn't on the other side of the house. I liked pretending; it was fun. The scolding ended when Papa said he would pay for the broken window.

Tauno's mother took the ruined pie with broken bits of glass outdoors and then went into the pantry. Smiling triumphantly, she came out with another apple pie in her hands and said, "I always bake at least four pies at a time." Placing the pie on the table, she added, "Saves wood, you know."

After the pie was cut, we kids were given a slice of it on a plate with a fork. We went outside and sat on the porch and ate while our parents had their coffee and pie indoors, sitting at the table next to the broken window. The pie tasted good, but my thoughts were elsewhere. I wondered whether, if I'd been a boy, I would have been able to throw the "ball" over the roof to reach make-believe Andy. It was a fun game. Someday I would throw a real ball over the roof for a make-believe Andy.

I liked the taste of cinnamon and sugar on the crust of the pie as much as the apples within. I wondered when we would have apple trees. My thoughts flew to birds that made nests on branches of trees. If I'd been a bird, I could have flown over the roof of the house and dropped the "ball" into Andy's hand, but, of course, Andy wasn't there. As I chewed and swallowed the tasty apple pie on my plate, I suddenly realized my plate was empty. I would have liked to have eaten another piece of pie. I didn't dare to ask for more. I was just a kid and a visitor who had ruined a whole pie.

I enjoyed watching birds fly. Sometimes they splashed their droppings on the clothes that Mama had washed. Since we didn't have a clothesline yet, she spread the washed sheets and towels over the bushes. I helped her sometimes. When the clothes were dry, she had me rub off the dried droppings. I could hardly see the spot where it had landed. I liked birds, even though they made work for me. They flew and they sang, but I liked Mama's singing better. At least I could understand what she said. Different birds had their own chirps, like people who come from different countries sing and talk their in own peculiar way.

One day I found an empty vanilla extract bottle that had been thrown down the incline next to the privy. It became my bird as I ran around the house. I tried chirping like a bird, but I wasn't sure which bird I was mimicking. I tried them all. After a while I wanted to put my bird to rest so I found dried grass and leaves. I molded them into a lump and shoved the pile into a corner of the house where the nest was protected by both walls. I had no trouble finding little pebbles among the hundreds of rocks that lay around. The pebbles became eggs and my bottle-bird was the mama who sat on the eggs. Since she had to leave her nest to catch insects, I flew her all over our yard, after which I returned her to the eggs. My bottle-bird and I did this for days and days. I finally got tired because the pebbles didn't hatch. I knew they couldn't; I had only been pretending.

Shortly after Papa had finished putting up the inside walls that covered the two-by-fours, he had gone to work on Highway 99 between Woodland and Kalama to earn money for the mortgage payment. One evening Mama suggested we play teeter-totter, which other people called seesaw. Mama fetched a long plank and placed it on top of the sawhorse that lay next to the woodshed. We had to adjust it several times before it would balance with both Helvi and me on the same side and Mama on the other.

That was the most musical evening I'd ever experienced! Mama sang folk songs from the old country. The stars popped out one by one. As the minutes ticked by, the sky darkened and the stars became brighter. Mama's voice was the only sound on the hill. No birds chirped. No cows lowed. No dogs barked. No cats crawled on the grassy slope. The silence was broken by Mama's voice as the stars sparkled down upon us. Helvi's arms circled tightly around me as we went up and down. Our feet barely touched the ground as we rose and dipped to the familiar tunes that comforted us under the magic of millions of lights overhead.

It was a shock to hear Mama stop singing and declare it was bedtime. Playtime was over. Our evening of wondrous sky gazing and comforting music stopped.

Many of the kids at school played drop the handkerchief. Each class stayed in its own group. It would have been nice to play games with the big kids in the second grade, but they thought we were too young. My teacher was Miss Goerig. Her parents had been pioneers in town so the main street leading into town was named after her family. She was a good teacher because she was strict, just like Mama.

Miss Goerig instructed us to drop the handkerchief behind someone who seldom had it dropped behind them. There were 27 of us in the class so our circle was large. When the handkerchief was dropped behind me, I could usually catch the person who would then have to go to the center of the circle. When it was my turn, I dropped it behind a boy who had not been chosen, just like Miss Goerig had told us to do. He just stared ahead and did not turn to see if the hanky had been dropped behind him so the person in the center grabbed it and ran after me. That poor boy had to go to the center of the ring.

I don't think he was happy that I had dropped the hanky behind him. He looked dazed and helpless as he stood turning around like a top but not watching where the hanky was dropped. He didn't know he was supposed to run inside the ring as the runner ran outside the ring. That way he could scoop up the hanky the moment it was dropped.

I think Miss Goerig was wrong to include everybody in the game. Although she was smart, she didn't know how it felt to be slow at catching on. The boy didn't understand, and he didn't enjoy being in the center of the ring like the rest of us did. I had made him look silly. I wasn't ashamed of having chosen him for I had done what I had been told, but I would never do it again.

Papa had told us what happened to Indians in our country. I felt sorry for people like them. Since nobody wanted to play Indians, I told Mama I would like to have one of the gunnysacks that had been emptied of grain and washed. I wanted to make an Indian girl's costume out of it. "If you make it yourself," she consented, "you may have one." It took no time at all for me to cut a hole at the bottom end for my head and slits on both sides for my arms. I was ready to play at being an Indian princess. I wanted to get some long chicken feathers to stick in my hair, but Mama wouldn't let me have any for she was saving them to make a pillow. It was just as well. I didn't think Indians had white Leghorn chickens. They used all kinds of colored feathers from wild birds. Well then, if I couldn't be an Indian princess, I'd be just an ordinary Indian maiden.

Walking up the hill after school one day, Tauno said several of the boys down the hill would come over to our place to play cowboys and Indians on Saturday. When they came, I put on my Indian dress. I looked like a real Indian even though I didn't have any feathers. Since none of the boys had guns like cowboys did, they brought their homemade bows and arrows. Mama reminded them to be careful since it was dangerous to play with them. They promised Mama they would be careful. We were only going to play.

The game began when the boys ordered me to run. I did; I ran as fast as I could. Behind me voices called, "Bang! Bang!" as arrows hit the dirt behind me. I heard someone yell,

"You're shot!" Other voices commanded, "You gotta lie down and die!" I ran to the top of the hill and stood facing the boys. They came huffing and puffing as I laughed and shouted, "This Indian maid lived through the massacre!" With my hands on my hips, I stood my ground. The boys were disgusted. They said it was no fun to play with a girl who didn't know how cowboys and Indians should be played.

I knew better. Papa had told me about the way Indians had been treated, so I knew the whites had not played fair with them. I couldn't change history, but I could change the way the game should be played! After picking up their arrows, the boys left to shoot some birds. I was glad I hadn't told them about my bottle-bird, which was still sitting on her stone eggs in the corner of the house.

I took off my costume and never put it on again. Mama used it later outside the door to wipe the mud off our shoes on rainy days. Sometimes I still thought of myself as a lovely Indian maid escaping the clutches of white men. My thoughts were often interrupted by Mama telling me to inform Papa to come for afternoon coffee or to eat. As I ran, I practiced what I would do when I grew up. Sometime in my future, Olympics would be held where real Indians could compete.

Playing cowboys and Indians made me disgusted with boys. I didn't want to be a boy anymore even if boys were stronger. Muscles looked great on men and horses, but it made me feel weak when Tauno did four pull-ups on a bar that his Papa had set up for him. Tauno didn't have to work like I did because his parents did not have a mortgage so he had more time to play and exercise to build up his muscles. Once I tried to do a pull-up on Tauno's bar. I barely made it up. My chin touched the iron bar, and then I dropped down with a thud. Tauno laughed, "You're supposed to come down slowly!" That wasn't fun; it wasn't a game so I left just like the boys did after playing cowboys and Indians. That made us even. So there!

Before Modern Conveniences

At school the teachers told us what to play at recess. I liked playing London Bridge; we had a chance to choose what we wanted. Two girls faced each other and held their hands up high, making a bridge, while others walked underneath as we chanted, "London Bridge is falling down, falling down, falling down on my fair lady." As soon as we said those words, the two girls dropped their hands around the person who was passing under the "bridge." She had to choose either peppermint or licorice and then line up behind the girl whose choice she had picked.

Even though I wasn't sure where London Bridge was, I had the chance to "make" it with my arms. My partner chose a stick of licorice and I chose peppermints because that's what Papa sometimes brought home after trips to town. In the game of London Bridge, we didn't tell the girl we caught under our bridge which goodie each of us had chosen. After all the girls had chosen either licorice or peppermints, we ended up with just about the same number of girls behind us. Then the fun began! Each girl linked arms around the waist of the one ahead and we had a tug of war. We tugged and tugged. The winning side would be the one that pulled the other side farthest. We pepperminters were mostly farm girls and we were at the point of being able to drag the other side farthest when the recess bell rang. That stopped our play. It was fun, not at all like doing pull-ups on a bar.

Unless a teacher was around, some of the boys spent their time trying to pick fights. I thought they would have liked to have us girls watch how strong they were as their fists aimed at each other's nose, but none of us girls liked to look at bloody noses.

Sometimes we'd play hide and seek at school. For some reason most of the boys didn't like to take part. I heard one kid say it was a girls' game. The game had nothing to do with being a boy or a girl. It was like being a detective! Furthermore, to get to the base before the one who had found you got there, you had to be a good runner. It was like training for the Olympics. I liked that.

I read a note one boy asked me to pass to another in class. He had spelled "kick" and "can" phonetically, just the way the words sounded. (That's how Finnish words were written, and he wasn't Finnish!) Although it wasn't easy, I thought boys should learn to spell the English way.

When I was a little older I sometimes watched the boys play kick the can. It looked rough. Very few kids had cans to bring to school and somehow the cans they brought with them got lost. It was obvious that boys didn't know how to save. Papa said he needed his oil cans to lubricate parts of the field machinery, just like Mama needed her Three-in-One can to insert oil in the moving parts of the Singer sewing machine. Glass jars, on the other hand, were used for canning year after year. No sensible person would go around kicking glass jars.

During lunch hour when we had more time, I found it pleasant to talk with my friends, who were Finns like me. We used to walk around the running track and chat about everything that interested us. One girl had many brothers. I liked to hear her talk about the silly things they did. We giggled and laughed about their activities because neither of us was interested in boys.

One sunny day someone suggested we play hopscotch on the narrow concrete walk in front of our school that led toward town. From somewhere chalk appeared, with which hopscotch squares were drawn. You had to kick a small wooden square to another square, but if it landed on a line, you would be out of the game. Some girls had difficulty balancing and kicked the block only an inch away so most of us just waited the whole recess period without getting a chance to play.

The next day rain had washed the hopscotch squares away and nobody had any chalk. That kind of a game was much too slow for me so I didn't care. Action games suited me better. After that, whenever it rained we simply walked around in the basement with our friends or played jump rope, which we all enjoyed. When someone didn't trip over the rope, we'd turn it faster and faster. That did it: turn time!

Sometimes we sat on the wooden bleachers next to the track and watched the boys play. It didn't look like play. Most of the time they just tried to knock each other down. Once in a while two boys would get into a real fight. That's when other boys stopped whatever they were doing and formed a circle around the fighters. Eventually a teacher on the grounds would come to stop the fighting.

I thought boys didn't have much sense because they liked to fight. We never found out why they got so mad at one another. Men knew better than boys; that's why Papa left Finland, so he wouldn't have to fight in the czar's army and be sent to Siberia. The boys in our school were only sent to the principal's office and that was in the same building. That's why they didn't care; it wasn't Siberia.

We received several catalogs every year: a special spring catalog and another in the fall. They came free in the mail. Helvi and I would cut pictures of people out of the catalogs. We made up stories about what our ladies and gentlemen did. I thought my stories were better than Helvi's. Her people talked like Mama and Papa, but my cutouts weren't always Finns. Sometimes they traveled to far-off places that we had read about at school. I had them talk that way too—even though I didn't know what they were saying. That's what happens when one goes to another country and hasn't learned to speak the language. If I ever went to Finland, I would be able to talk to people like Helvi's paper people, but I preferred to hear our teacher talk English like everyone else in Woodland except the Finnish people who went to the hall.

One summer I earned enough money from picking strawberries to order a pair of bedroom slippers. Then, when I got up in the morning and had to do my business outdoors, my feet didn't get cold. (We had long since stopped using the pot under the bed.) My bedroom slippers were so comfortable I danced with them on. Riitta, my friend down the hill, liked to dance also. We both liked acrobatics and dancing. We had seen the type of poses dancers did because the druggist in town gave us unsold dance magazines. Pictures of Isadora Duncan, an American dancer, and Pavlova, a Russian ballet dancer, intrigued us.

Riitta made a glade for dancing among the trees and shrubs next to the barn. Her papa sowed seeds there so we danced on grass. We believed we were good dancers as we flung our hands and kicked our legs this way and that with pointed toes like ballet dancers. We felt graceful. Riitta had long hair that sometimes got in her way. My hair had been cut in the second grade so it never got in my eyes.

I also made a dancing glade past our pig pen where there were a lot of birch trees and undergrowth. It was hard work clearing the brush and fallen branches. After several afternoons of work, I paused and really looked at my project. I saw that it was not as nice as Riitta's dancing glade. I didn't want to spend time there anymore even though I had worked so hard to clean it up. Besides, it was too close to the stinking pig pen. Why hadn't I noticed that before?! Mama said I should think twice before I did anything. I had at least cleared a shady spot for the cattle. I didn't show Riitta what I had done. Instead, we danced in her glade.

Then we decided to make crepe paper costumes and have a picture taken. Helvi had a box camera and she said she'd take one picture. Riitta's paper dress was bright red. It looked really nice with her black hair. My costume was white paper to show off my tan. We each made a crown for ourselves. Riitta's crown was taller than mine, but I didn't mind. Hers tipped back and forth when she moved. Mine stayed firmly upright, the way I thought a crown should.

When our picture was taken, I wore my new bedroom slippers. They felt comfortable and warm and soft, not at all like the pebbles and stickers that my bare feet endured on my daily trips around the barn and fields. I felt sorry for Riitta because she wore her old black everyday slippers with the strap over her instep. I felt light as a feather and I imagined I looked as dainty as a fairy. Anyway, that was the way I felt. Riitta admired my slippers with the fluffy tassel on top.

While waiting for the roll of film to be developed, we danced and did acrobatics whenever we were able to get together. Helvi didn't watch us dance like Pavlova or Isadora Duncan. She said our cartwheels, headstands and splits were silly stunts to get attention. Mama knew my dancing kept me out of Helvi's way in the kitchen so she said it was OK to run to Riitta's whenever my work was done. And run I did!

Finally, when the film was developed, I couldn't believe how I looked—not at all how I had felt at the time! My bedroom slippers didn't look as nice as Riitta's black slippers did. Neither did our skirts stand out like a ballet dancer's; they hung straight down. We were both so disappointed with our pictures that neither of us wore those outfits again. We didn't pretend to be Pavlova or Isadora Duncan anymore. We just switched to acrobatics.

An older girl named Jenny went to school with us. She was special; I liked to mimic the way she walked because she was handicapped. It was sort of a game with me. One reason I admired her was because her parents were rich. They had come to this country with money and paid cash for their farm. Jenny did not wear thick long underwear like we did that made her stockings bulge. She also had leather gloves. Sears and Ward's only sold woolen and cotton gloves. Heavy cotton gloves were for work. Mama said they were canvas gloves. Papa bought them from the co-op in town and they wore out quickly because he had so much work to do. The leather gloves that Jenny wore stayed nice and smooth all winter, but then she didn't play in the snow like the rest of us did. She hung on the arm of her neighbor friend as they walked to the school bus. She'd had some serious disease when she was a baby. Her right ankle touched the ground and she flung her left leg, but she was very pretty and wore clothes ordered from catalogs. I was sure her leather gloves were the fashion everywhere in the world.

One day Mama saw me walking like Jenny. She told me to stop. "I can't explain why, Miriami, but I don't think you should walk like Jenny." She paused a moment, then added, "Somebody might think you're making fun of her." I couldn't figure that out. I had tried to act like her because she had leather gloves, wore store-bought dresses and did not wear long underwear. Why would anyone think I was making fun of her?! Helvi also told me to stop and added, "You should be ashamed!" Both Mama and Helvi thought what I was doing was exactly the opposite of the way I felt. Their remarks made me recall the snapshot of Riitta and me so I didn't walk like Jenny anymore—although I really had wished I could be like her. People made mistakes when they thought they could read my mind. I believed I was something special, especially when I walked like Jenny or pretended to be a ballerina, but I was neither.

Jenny had given Helvi a pack of old greasy cards. Her parents had purchased a new set of cards that slid well on the kitchen oilcloth. That's how wealthy they were! When we had visited her home, she had taught us how to play solitaire as well as steal the pack. We didn't tell Mama that we had cards. We thought playing cards was just a game. We had a feeling, however, that Mama would think it was a waste of time because it wasn't working or studying.

One day Mama caught us playing cards. She got very angry and shouted, "I didn't come from Finland to have my daughters playing cards like men in saloons!" She whisked the cards from under our surprised eyes, walked to the stove, opened the firebox lid, and dropped them into the fire. That was the end of that game.

Whenever we went to the neighbors for a sauna, however, the men played pinochle after they had bathed. They enjoyed it and they hadn't been drinking anything but coffee—and they weren't in a saloon! Grown-ups were hard to figure out. Mama thought cards wasted time and that people should read and learn in their spare time, but men found cards relaxing after a day's hard labor. Even friends of our parents didn't think alike. Every person was different. That's why people argued so much in their spare time.

Whenever we bought anything from the co-op, it was placed in a paper bag and tied with string. Mama saved all the string from those packages and rolled it into a ball. One day when Tauno came over, I asked Mama if we could have the ball of string so we could play with it. She tucked the loose end into the ball and let me have it. I suggested we just play catch. All went well until I threw the ball of string into a fresh pile of cow manure. I had forgotten that our cows had been in the yard that morning to eat the grass. I felt awful, just as

Before Modern Conveniences

bad as when I had thrown the hard ball of clay through the window onto the fresh apple pie. Now I had thrown a ball of string into another soft deposit. For reasons of her own, Mama did not scold me. Since she believed in saving everything, she washed and cleaned the messy ball herself.

Helvi thought the end of my catch game was funny. She and I thought differently—like grown-ups did so much of the time. Tauno was disgusted with me and went home. I didn't care. Playing any kind of ball game was not my kind of fun. I was going to run in the Olympics!

8

School Days

It was the happiest day of my life as I trudged down Butte Hill with my sister and dozens of others going to school: I was going into first grade! We chatted excitedly while waiting for the school bus on its journey up the Lewis River. Besides my lunch bucket, I carried a bundle of supplies that Mama had wrapped for me. In it was the first grade reader that Papa had purchased half price at the drugstore. The thick five-cent tablet and one-cent pencil came from the co-op. The pencil had an eraser on one end so it could be used to wipe out mistakes, but I didn't intend to make any mistakes! I was sure of that.

    I had watched Papa the evening before as he had sharpened Helvi's and my pencils. He reached for the knife from his overall pocket and dug out a blade. While holding the pencil in his left hand, he slowly and methodically turned the wooden stem while slicing the wood into thin strips tapering to the lead tip of the pencil. When he had finished, it was as sharp as the needles Mama used on the Singer sewing machine. I wanted to use the pencil right away as it was a big change from the thin stick I used on the slate that Papa had given us a long time ago. But Papa said the tablet and pencil were for school. The slate was for scribbling. That hurt my feelings because I knew the alphabet and put letters together that Helvi had taught me. That wasn't scribbling!

Although only part of the large Butte Hill crowd, I felt special as I stood clutching my book, tablet, pencil and lunch; I was ready for school. What an adventure, riding a bus every day!

We entered the bus from the front. It seemed as if a wind had struck us as the bus driver sped ahead at 30 miles an hour on a straightaway. Our horse had never run so fast! To keep the wind from hitting us directly, both sides of the bus were covered with tacked-on, removable heavy canvas. Our bus was really a truck that had wooden benches installed on each side and in the middle. I sat at the side so I could see everybody else. Helvi and I wore our best clothes, the same ones we wore when we went to the Finn hall. We never wore our good clothes at home. As soon as we got home, we hung them on hooks in the clothes closet. I remember when Papa replaced the nails with hooks. We were going up in the world! Someday we would have clothes hangers, Papa promised. Wearing my Finn hall clothes to school meant this was life at its very best and I must behave like a student.

Helvi had shown me the year before where first grade was located so I felt like a grown-up walking alone to the door. Miss Goerig greeted me nicely just like she greeted all the other kids. We sat wherever we wanted. Naturally my two Finnish girlfriends took seats as close to me as they could. There were three Finnish boys in this class of 27 and they also sat together as boys should. I didn't know if my friends knew English, but I understood what Miss Goerig said when she asked our names. Huttunen is a real Finnish name so she didn't know how to write it. Since I knew the letters of the alphabet, I spelled it out loud for her. My friends didn't have to spell their names because they had been

Americanized by adding the ending "son." I was surprised when the students who spoke English didn't know the alphabet.

Miss Goerig asked us all to stand near the windows that formed two sides of the room. Then she seated us alphabetically according to our last names. That separated groups of friends, including us. Miss Goerig told us not to whisper so I didn't. (At least we could talk to one another during recess. That was enough talking time when one was going to school.) We often talked in Finnish at recess and the other kids didn't like that. They thought we were talking about them—sometimes that was true.

After a few days of reading from a book about family and pets, Miss Goerig put us into different reading groups. We three girls were separated again. I didn't like that, but the teacher was the boss, just like Mama was at home. It had to be that way because there were so many of us. We had to keep our mouths shut so we could hear her. If we chattered like we did at home, it would sound like the cackling and crowing around the chicken coop. The teacher didn't say that; I just knew how hens and roosters sounded when they got excited.

One day Miss Goerig gave each of us a narrow colored slip of paper. She told us to keep it below each line we were reading so our eyes would stay on the sentence. She sat on a chair in front of the class when she called us to read. We were told to stand beside her in front of the entire class. (That was like performing at the Finn hall!) Some kids were shy and hung their heads; others blushed. Some didn't want to read because they had trouble even if they held the colored strip underneath each line.

One day a boy went up to Miss Goerig during the reading session and told her he had lost his strip of paper. That gave me an idea. If I had enough of those strips, I could paste them together and make a Christmas tree chain! So I slipped my strip on the shelf under the desktop where my tablet lay and went up to get a new one. She gave it to me. Shortly afterwards I went up and interrupted another kid's reading. I asked for a strip. She looked somewhat surprised but gave me one. I was really happy because it was a different color! After a few minutes I went up the third time to ask for a strip. Miss Goerig didn't hand me one. Instead, she said in a firm but quiet voice, "Go sit on the trunk in the corner until recess time." I hadn't whispered! I had asked her in a quiet voice.

I sat on the trunk where she kept supplies: crayons, colored paper, books, pencils, paint sets and scissors. A few days earlier a boy had whispered in class and had been sent to sit on the trunk and now I was sitting on the same trunk. I didn't think I had done anything wrong like whispering. Of course, she didn't know that I wanted to make a chain for our Christmas tree at home like we had the previous year. How would she know, I figured. She wasn't Finnish!

I knew everything in the trunk cost money. I wondered if she had spent her own money to buy the colored paper from which she made the reading strips for us. Maybe she had a mortgage like Mama and Papa had. I thought teachers got very good pay because their work was much more important than plowing or milking cows. Even if she got good pay, she shouldn't use her own money to make it easier for us to read. Those thoughts began to make me feel guilty, but as soon as the recess bell rang, I jumped off the trunk and I felt OK. Neither of my friends had noticed that Miss Goerig had sent me to the corner. (I was pleased they had their noses in the reader.) I did not tell them what had happened.

One day a new girl came to class. Everybody noticed her because she was barefoot. While most of us went barefoot at home during the summer, none of us went to school without shoes. Some of the kids did have holes in their stockings, especially boys if they didn't have sisters to darn the stockings or their Mamas were too busy to do so. My stockings were always darned; Mama saw to that. The barefoot girl's name was Nellie, and she was very, very skinny—much skinnier than I. She coughed a lot, a dry hacking cough, not the kind that you have when you have a cold with a snotty nose. Maybe she had a lung disease like a lot of the Finn farmers who had previously worked in the mines. They called it "miner's gone," a short way of saying they would die. But Nellie had not worked in the mines; she was just a girl like me. She couldn't be sick that way. I felt sorry for her. At the first recess I went up to her and asked her to walk around the track with me. I told her what my name was and she told me hers, but I knew it already because Miss Goerig had introduced her to the class. I was not forgetful.

I learned that Nellie's papa worked in the big sawmill that stood at the edge of town. She told me that they were poor so I told her we were poor, too, but she could see that we all wore shoes and she didn't. I wondered if her papa was a drinker. Mama said that drinkers spent their money in saloons and let their kids and wives go without proper food or clothes. I ate a lot and I was still skinny, but not like Nellie. I thought her bones would rattle as we walked, but I didn't hear any noise.

Nellie tagged onto me day after day during recess, but she went home during the lunch hour. When she returned one day, I offered her a piece of cardamom biscuit. She ate it so fast that I knew she was still hungry. When I told Mama about Nellie being so skinny and coming barefoot to school, Mama was pleased that I was nice to her. She put an extra slice of cardamom biscuit into my lunch bucket the next day for Nellie and I also gave her an apple.

My lunch was put into an old lard bucket. Mama mixed lard with flour to make the bottom and top crusts of apple pies. She made pies all winter until the apples were gone. Even the apples that were half rotten were used. Mama just cut the spoiled part off. She didn't believe anyone should waste anything.

One day one of my Finnish friends looked at my lunch, was surprised and said, "You have a lot of good food." I saw she had only two slices of bread with bacon grease! I had a pint jar of milk, a sandwich with butter, a slice of apple pie wrapped in wax paper, a small container of apple sauce and a whole apple. Since she thought I had a lot of food, I offered her the apple sauce and told her to return the spoon and container as soon as she was through eating. She was just like all of us, sometimes forgetful, so I let her know that I wasn't giving away things I had to take home or Mama would scold me. I thought she looked jealous as she spooned up the apple sauce and I didn't offer her any of my pie. I had trouble with the pie. It was difficult to eat because I had to keep the wax paper folded underneath. I could have used the spoon I had given her with which to eat the apple sauce. I told her I would let her have a bite of my apple pie the next day, if Mama would make another one. When we were both through eating, I let her have a bite of my apple as we walked around the track. I liked to share, but not too much.

All of us put our lunch buckets under the hook in the hallway where we hung our sweaters or coats. Although a lot of other kids also carried their lunch in lard buckets, mine was different; Mama had scratched my name on the side. Very few carried their lunch in a paper sack. I couldn't figure out where they got so many sacks. I envied them; they didn't have to carry a bucket home.

Leaving the school bus and walking up the hill, sometimes the jar and spoon would rattle as I jumped over the rocks on the road. We started a game that one of the older boys said he had learned in class. Holding the handle, we would quickly spin our bucket over our head round and round as fast as we could. Nothing rattled! The boy said that everything stayed at the bottom of the bucket, just like human beings on Earth. We didn't fly into space even if we were upside down on the other side of the sun at night. The earth rolled much faster, he said, than our lard buckets, but the idea was the same. That's what the grown-up eighth-grader told us. He called it "sentrifewgl" force. I searched for the word in my little black dictionary, but I couldn't find it under *s* as in strawberries. Then I remembered the two-cent stamps I used on the letters to my cousins so I looked under *c*. After leafing through several pages, I found a word that meant the same, but it was spelled "centrifugal." Spelling in English isn't as sensible as in Finnish.

Even though I had learned why my jar and spoon didn't rattle when I twirled the bucket, I got tired of swinging my hand around so that ended the game for me. But I did learn a grown-up eighth-grade word while doing it so it was worth the experience. And I knew now that my feet were above my head at night even if it didn't feel that way. I stayed put, with my feet on the ground, just like the contents at the bottom of my lard bucket.

One day I found a note that a big boy at school had tossed on the ground, but the spelling of the word that meant making babies was wrong. Being older didn't mean being smarter, especially in spelling. I learned quite a bit by listening to older girls who knew how to spell that word.

I liked the holidays because we had a chance to draw pumpkins at Thanksgiving and pictures of Santa Claus in December. I knew that mamas and papas were the real Santas, but it was fun to pretend. I was surprised that some of my classmates really believed in the white-bearded, red-coated man from the North. When I told Mama, she warned me not to contradict them. She said that was what their parents had told them and it would not be OK to correct my classmates. She constantly told me not to talk too much. I don't know why; that's what she and the teacher did.

I liked to draw Pilgrims. Papa said the Indians fed the Pilgrims the first winter; otherwise, they would have starved. The Pilgrims did not force their religion on the Indians because they knew what it felt like to believe what the government ordered. Maybe that's why I wasn't allowed to tell a boy in my class there was no Santa Claus. But Santa wasn't a religion; he was just a make-believe man that made the Christmas story interesting by giving gifts to the good kids.

I knew what a play was. It was a story put into action. Miss Goerig had us perform a play about Mistress Mary and most of the kids were chosen to act like flowers. They didn't have to say anything. All they did was sway in the breeze. She chose me as Miss Crosspatch and I was allowed to say something. I stomped my foot and told a few of the characters they didn't know anything about taking care of plants. It would have been better to get the part of Mistress Mary because that was the best part. I was jealous, but I kept my mouth shut to stay out of trouble. Mama would have been proud of me. I never told her I wanted the best part so she was satisfied with the part Miss Goerig gave me in the play.

One night it snowed so much that Mama wouldn't let me go to school in the morning. She let Helvi go. I didn't think that was fair. I could stomp through the snow just as well as she could. It was like going on a hike and stepping over a fallen log, but different. I told Mama she didn't know how important going to school was because she had never gone to school in the old country. That's when she got so angry with me that I was afraid she was going to pull my hair. (She did that now and then.) Instead, she turned around and got ready to go to the barn. That's when she told me that for punishment I had to stay in the house. She wouldn't even allow me to get a kitten to play with. Going to the barn would have given me a chance to show I could walk in snow just as well as she and Helvi.

I watched the kitchen clock tick as an hour went by. Mama came into the house with a bucket of milk and poured some into a pitcher and the rest into a bowl. I didn't really watch what she did as I was still annoyed with her for not letting me go to school. My anger was gone the moment I saw Helvi coming down the ridge. She had been gone three hours! I was glad I could tell time; some of the kids in class still couldn't do so. They would say that the little hand was on such-and-such a number and the big hand was on another number. I used to do that too when I was a kid.

Helvi said she and a couple of others from Butte Hill had waited and waited for the bus to come, but it never did so they returned home. I was glad there was no school because I didn't like to miss a day. One of the reasons Papa and Mama had come to this country was to have us educated, but I also liked riding the school bus!

We usually did not talk much while walking downhill to get to the school bus. (We didn't want to be late.) One morning, however, Tauno remarked that there was an unusual bird flying in the distance and it sounded as if it was making a noise. We stopped walking. It looked different. It couldn't be a bird. It was a machine! That's when Helvi said it might be one of those new airplanes used in World War I that Papa had read about some time ago. Well, there was no war going on so we didn't need to be afraid.

We had seen pictures of airplanes but hadn't seen one flying. We spent the remainder of the time walking to the bus stop wondering where the plane had come from and where it was headed. Most of the older kids believed it came from Portland and was flying north to Seattle. We couldn't figure out what was inside: people, baggage or supplies? Couldn't trains take care of all transportation? Surely they were safer than the possibility of falling from an airplane? That airplane was the topic of conversation on the bus as well as at school during recess and lunchtime.

I was proud to enter the second grade. One of the girls who lived in town had a beautiful red cape instead of a coat. Her uncle was the town barber. I thought they were rich. That sort of cape must have cost a lot of money. It had two slits so she could put her hands out, but usually she didn't. She let the cape drape around her body. At Christmastime she looked like Santa's little girl until she took off her cape and hung it on a hook like all of us had to do. That red woolen cape just wouldn't look right marching up the hill with our raincoats. I had become quite sensible, like a grown-up. I could now think like one!

Our teacher taught us arithmetic. When we had learned addition, she sent two of us to the board. The first one to add the problems written on the board correctly had a star marked beside his or her name on the far side of the blackboard. I was pleased with all the stars I had, but I felt bad that some of the kids didn't have any stars. No wonder my Finnish friends didn't like school. I wouldn't have either if I had had no stars next to my name. They had a hard time memorizing numbers. It wasn't easy for me, either, but I kept repeating the answers until they stuck in my head, or somewhere between my ears. Everything takes time, even memorizing numbers. Mama kept telling Helvi and me to learn something new every day. That meant arithmetic problems, too.

The boy who sat at the end of my row was Gordon. I liked him. He was different. Freckles covered his face! He never looked at me. I had no business looking around the classroom, but once in a while I did take a quick look at him. His freckles were dark tan like a spotted brown and tan barn cat we once had. Tauno, my neighbor, had rosy cheeks but no freckles. He ate his oatmeal mush every morning, at least that's what Mama said. I ate oatmeal mush every morning, but I didn't have rosy cheeks or freckles. I didn't dare ask Gordon what he ate to get all those freckles. He had a sister in the first grade, but I didn't want to ask about her brother's freckles. Sisters were silly and couldn't keep secrets. I knew all about sisters.

I had a hard time getting permission from Mama to go downtown to the co-op to buy a new pair of shoes. Papa had put half soles on my high-buttoned shoes, but the soles were worn out again. Mama knew they were also getting too small for me. Besides, I liked the new style of laced shoes. If I had that kind of shoe, I wouldn't have to hunt around the house for the button hook to get my shoes buttoned. I complained a lot that my shoes pinched my toes. Mama finally gave me permission to go to the store. She insisted, however, that I eat my lunch before going to town. She ought to have known that I'd never skip eating. Not eat? I was always hungry!

I gobbled my lunch, like a hog Mama would have said, and ran to the store, which was just two blocks away from school. Lempi, the clerk, was busy in the shoe corner cleaning eggs that some farmer had brought. She stopped her work long enough to measure the length and width of my foot. Then she climbed a ladder and took down several boxes of shoes. They were all Buster Brown shoes with laces!

Lempi had to leave me for a while because a farmer had come in who gave her a grocery list that his wife had written. Lempi told me to go ahead and try on the shoes. In the meantime, she began to get the supplies for the man to take home.

Meanwhile, the man went to join others who were sitting around the pot-bellied stove talking about crops, cooperatives and politics. They were interested in the new world even if they weren't citizens. They all wanted to be citizens but didn't have time to study American history or government like Papa had many years ago. He had taken part in a Minnesota iron-ore strike in 1907, which the miners lost. All the strikers were blacklisted; he couldn't get a job. That's when he went to the Work People's College and learned enough English and studied many other subjects so that he was able to get his citizenship. Papa was proud of that. He had opinions on everything because he had read so much. When Papa went to the co-op, he also liked to sit around the pot-bellied stove and talk, but he wasn't there now. I was buying my own pair of laced shoes without anyone hovering over me!

When Lempi returned to her egg-cleaning job and me, I told her which pair I wanted and she put them into the box. Mama had written a note giving me permission to get the shoes so Lempi let me take the box to school.

That evening I proudly put on my new pair of shoes. While strutting back and forth in our kitchen, Papa said something sounded wrong. Mama stopped what she was doing and gazed at my shoes. She exclaimed, "Miriami, one shoe has a rubber heel and the other has a wooden heel!" Looking up from the book she was reading, Helvi snickered. I sat down on a chair and looked at my shoes. Studying them carefully, I saw they did have a slightly different cut on top. Otherwise, they were identical in color—brown, as I had wanted—and they were laced shoes, not buttoned shoes. That's all I cared about and I said so. Mama sighed and said I must pick one or the other; she would go to town the next day and make the proper exchange.

I had a difficult time deciding which heel I preferred. After a lot of thinking, I decided to have the wooden heels so people could hear me coming and going. From then on, the only thing Mama allowed me to buy during my lunch hour was fresh yeast to make bread or a spool of cotton thread for the sewing machine. I didn't even have much choice of colors because Mama only wanted two colors, either white or black. I could remember that easily. My friends seldom wanted to go to the store with me, but I didn't care. I enjoyed the click of the wooden heels of my laced shoes as I ran along the sidewalk thinking of the Olympics!

In the third grade I learned a lot during recess and noon from one of my classmates. She was a Lutheran girl who hated Catholics. She told me that they did not believe in the right kind of God. I didn't know there was a right and a wrong God. Neither did she, but that's what she had been told. She said a man who helped on their farm was a Catholic and he was not a good person. "Why isn't he a good person?" I asked once. She didn't really know, she said. Maybe it was because sometimes when he came into the house he was very dirty from field work. He didn't wash his hands before he came to the table. My Papa didn't always wash his hands when he came to eat either. He didn't want to waste water that Mama had carried a long distance. Papa wasn't a Catholic, I was sure, because I'd never heard him say that anyone was going to Hell even when he disagreed with them.

My schoolfriend said their Catholic hired hand ate the same kind of food she and her parents ate. I remembered Papa saying that we were mainly what we ate and not how we looked. I wondered if Catholics secretly ate other kinds of food to make them pray to a different God, but Mama said there was only one God. My classmate was OK even though we didn't have the same kind of food in our lunch buckets. Although I didn't know if I was a Lutheran or a Catholic, she didn't get mad at me. She liked the lunch I carried in my bucket with apple sauce, apple pie and also a whole apple. Sometimes it had a worm in it. I'd bite it off and spit it out for the birds. That wasn't wasting. The birds ate what I didn't. Was that being a Lutheran or a Catholic? I was glad I didn't have to declare myself. My friends liked me for what I was, even if I didn't know what I was. I couldn't understand why my Lutheran and Catholic classmates hated each other. I liked them all in a different way—they spoke English.

My third grade was not very interesting. Our teacher read to the class from books in the school library for 15 minutes every morning. Sometimes she read a book that only the boys liked. I didn't like those stories. That's when I thought maybe I didn't want to be a boy after all.

Other than being read to every single morning, all we seemed to do was learn the multiplication tables up to 12 times 12, which was 144. My two Finnish friends thought arithmetic was hard. They had to take the third grade over. They were slower at memorizing, that's all. I think it was wrong they had to stay in the same grade another year because they finally made it into the fourth grade. I didn't have them as my classmates anymore; I missed them.

Once, while hiking up the two-mile Butte Hill Road, I was laughed at and I didn't know why. The older kids were talking about having babies because one of the girls had said her mother was going to have one. An eighth-grade boy remarked that he had heard of an unmarried girl in town having a baby. That's when I raised my voice and shouted, "No girl can have a baby without being married!" The older kids laughed at me. Even the girls. I didn't like that.

As soon as we got home, Helvi told Mama how dumb I was. That's when Mama suddenly stopped puttering around the kitchen, told us to sit down and began a long story about girls having babies without a father for the child. She said that was not good for the baby. I thought everybody knew a married man was needed to do the hard outside work for the family.

Before I went into the fourth grade, Aunt Ida invited me to spend the summer with her in Portland. I think Mama was glad to have me gone and I was anxious to spend the summer in a big city. Aunt Ida had a huge house with an upstairs. I had a room to myself, but there wasn't a thing in it except the bed. And there was dust under the bed! I didn't dare say anything because it wouldn't be nice to say it should be cleaned. Naturally I didn't think of doing any housework because I wasn't very good at it. I was taught to keep the barn in order, but maybe dust under the bed was OK. It wasn't dirt like in barns.

Before Modern Conveniences

One day Aunt Ida saw scratches on the seat of the dining-room chair. She asked if I had made them. Of course not! She was puzzled. Later she saw me sitting with my legs balanced on the front of the seat of the chair. I heard a loud cry. "It's your shoes! The heels are leaving nail marks on my mahogany chair!" I knew better. They weren't her chairs. She'd got them when she'd married the old man whose wife had died. She'd inherited the chairs from that woman. Of course, nobody wants to have scratches on shiny brown furniture. I told her I was sorry and that I wouldn't sit with both legs perched on the seat of the chair anymore. I sat that way at home, but now I knew it was a bad habit. I was learning to sit like city folk!

One day Aunt Ida gave me a trowel. I had never seen one before; it looked like a small shovel. She told me to go outside and pull the weeds from the flower bed next to the house. I went outside and looked and looked. All I could see were lots of nice green plants. How was I to know what were flowers and what were weeds? We had nothing but a lilac bush in our yard.

Puzzled but obedient, I pulled out the largest and longest green plants as well as some of the small ones. When Aunt Ida came outside, a quick look let me know she was angry. She scolded me just like Mama! I didn't cry because I'd done my best. It was her fault; she should have shown me which ones were weeds. I liked the shovels on the farm. They were bigger than trowels and I could work standing up. Besides, it wasn't real work pulling weeds while kneeling.

I didn't think I gave Aunt Ida any real trouble, but I knew she wanted to get rid of me for a while because she had me stay at a hotel run by a friend of hers. The hotel was on Skid Row. They had a girl my age and a boy. The lady's husband was crippled with arthritis, but he was a good-natured man. Even though she was no relative, she treated me the same as her own daughter. Maybe that's why Aunt Ida was the way she was. She didn't have kids of her own. The girl's name was Irene and she had beautiful red hair and freckles over her nose and cheekbones, almost like the boy in the second grade. I thought Irene was the prettiest girl I had ever seen. She showed me how to swing on the rings in the nearby park! That was fun, even though we had to take turns with dozens of others.

Everything was different living with Aunt Ida's friends who were managers of a hotel on Burnside Street. The buildings were large and close together and there was a lot of noise. I was in the center of the city! The streetcars rushed by and when they stopped, people stepped out and others clambered into the cars. Everyone was in a hurry even though they had no cows or chickens to take care of. Maybe they just came into town to buy clothes. I wondered if they knew there was a Ward's store in town. Why didn't they order their clothes from Ward's and stay home instead of rushing around?

I enjoyed seeing the rose parade. A lot of well-dressed girls rode in cars and horses pranced in groups. The horses didn't look like the ones we had on the farm. Workhorses don't prance. I wondered where they kept those horses when they weren't parading and prancing. I couldn't keep my eyes off them because they reminded me of the one I had carved when our house was being built. If it had really been alive, I was sure my carved horse would have pranced just like those on parade. I kept my eyes on their tails and behinds even when they were far off and half hidden by bugles blowing and marching men.

A few days later, Aunt Ida came to visit. She had written Mama that I was staying in a hotel with her friend and Mama had replied that she didn't like my staying in a "red-light district" hotel, even if she was Ida's friend. I think Aunt Ida was glad to get rid of me because she had already packed my clothes when she came and led me to the bus depot with a ticket back to Woodland which she had bought.

My vacation was over. "All good things come to an end," Mama used to tell me. That was supposed to be a sad saying, but I was glad to get back home even though Mama scolded me. I did not like her city sister for not explaining what she wanted me to do. Mama explained too much, and I didn't like that either. Oh, well.

While riding home, I enjoyed watching the bus driver. He was businesslike. He wore a uniform. He called out the names of all the places where people were waiting for the bus. And he knew when someone wanted to get off; I supposed they had told him when they came on the Greyhound bus. I wondered if I could ever be a bus driver, but I was a girl, and driving was not for us even when we grew up. That was too bad. I thought I would look better in a uniform than the overalls I wore at home working in the barn. I thought of riding on a bus all day. Turning the steering wheel was not really work. I wondered if the driver ever had a chance to go to the toilet. I knew there was one in Woodland, but it was in the back room of the co-op. The bus didn't stop there. Otherwise, bus drivers had it easy and their work was clean. They didn't get dusty or dirty at the end of the day, but they might get miserable if they couldn't get to a toilet! I wondered where they went when they really had to go. I admired the uniform the bus driver wore. I would have liked one like that if I could have worn it in the barn.

I was glad to see Papa waiting for me right by the bus stop. He had already done his shopping at the co-op so we went home right away. He asked me if I had enjoyed visiting

Portland and I told him the truth about Aunt Ida. Papa laughed. "She doesn't understand children," he said. He knew I was eight years old and wasn't a child! He and Mama had both agreed that I should spend the summer in Portland with Mama's sister. Children weren't sent away from home. I was so happy to be with Papa that I didn't correct him. Actually, I never did contradict him; he was a man.

Instead of talking, I watched the horse plugging away. As I was getting hungry, I told Papa that I was anxious to get home. I complained that the horse walked sooooooo slowly. (I was also thinking of the prancing horses in the rose parade.) Papa said that I had never complained before about the speed of horses and he then added, "After riding streetcars and the bus, I suppose you feel like a city girl." Thoughtfully, as if talking to himself, he said, "You'll just have to get used to our slower country ways again." Saying this, he shook the reins slightly and the horse quickened its step.

Papa had lived in big towns and cities so he knew how I felt. He knew the difference between city and country life. He understood me! But I wondered if other towns had red-light districts like Portland had. I knew that Irene was happy living there and she was a good girl. The whole family was nice to me, much nicer than Mama's sister who lived in a big house and had a yard with several trees, lots of flowers and weeds that I hadn't pulled out.

The summer finally ended! We were so glad to be going to school that both Helvi and I ran down the hill to meet the school bus. I was going into the fourth grade, which was the highest grade on the second floor. The ground-level concrete basement was really the first floor of the school building. On rainy days we had to spend our recess and lunch periods in the basement, but we weren't allowed to run there.

I looked forward to the fourth grade because I had so much to tell my classmates about spending most of my summer in Portland. In the second and third grades the teachers had asked us kids to tell the class what we had done during the summer. Since most of us were farm kids, our stories both years were about the same thing. This year, however, I was going to surprise everyone with my Portland trip! Days went by, but our teacher didn't ask us to give an oral report of our summer activities. Weeks went by. In the meantime, several of my classmates had already heard about my wonderful summer vacation. I did not tell them about scratching my aunt's mahogany chair or pulling the plants out along with the weeds. That was not lying. I just omitted a part I didn't like.

One day at school I felt a sharp pain at the tip of my toe. Naturally it was impossible to take off my shoe; it took too much time to unlace. I just put up with the pain. That evening I took off my shoe and there was no pebble in it. Instead, the point of a nail was sticking out. Papa had ordered a sheet of leather from the mail order catalog the previous year and, whenever necessary, he repaired each and every one of our shoes. He cut the leather to the shape of the shoe and nailed it on.

Papa took the offending shoe to the corner of the kitchen where the anvil stood. He shoved the shoe onto the last and pounded the sole with a hammer. Handing the shoe back to me, he murmured, "Mirri can let the cat do the scratching from now on." He said it so low that Helvi didn't hear. He was joking. We didn't have mahogany chairs; it didn't matter how I sat! I was happy because my shoes still clicked when I walked with my solid wooden heels. And I could click better now that my toe didn't hurt.

I did tell stories about seeing the rose parade. Some of my friends did not even know what a parade was, so I told them! (That almost made me feel like a teacher.) I let them know that city kids had a lot of fun exercising in the parks. We didn't have a park in Woodland. Farm life was almost like a park, but not exactly the same. Everything kids did in parks was fun. On the farm we used as many muscles, but it was work. Was work different for Lutherans and Catholics? I wondered if you were a Lutheran, for example, you were one at church or at home, but not at the park. Or maybe you were one everywhere.

My fourth-grade teacher was a real old lady. She had a son in the eighth grade. I think her husband had died because married women weren't allowed to teach. Husbands had to provide for the family, like Papa did. I couldn't figure that out because farm women worked as hard as their husbands. Maybe it was different if women got a paycheck.

I thought it was wrong to keep married women from teaching. They could have told us something we ought to know about getting along with boys since they had first-hand knowledge of grown-up men. It was too bad that a man had to die before his wife could teach us kids.

Women's work on farms wasn't paid, but their work was worth money. Mama didn't get a paycheck, but she was always saying, "Do this," and "Do that," just to save money. Her work made savings, which helped Papa pay the mortgage.

Maybe my fourth-grade teacher had to write all the business letters because she insisted we learn to spell. Spelling was very important to her. We had spelling tests every week. I liked to write the words, but I got rattled when we had spelling bees. I couldn't see the words in my mind as I could when I wrote them. I wanted to be the last one up, to be the winner. I never was the winner. That made me disgusted because I always got a 100 on my spelling tests, but the kids in my class didn't know that unless I told them. If I did, it would sound as if I were bragging even if it was the truth. Mama was proud that I was good at the spelling tests and she told me that no one could be first at everything. But winning a spelling bee was much better than getting 100 in tests. The winner of a spelling bee didn't have to brag; kids could see who was the best. It was like having the lead part in a play at the Finn hall!

In the fifth grade we had a traveling singing teacher. He came to our school once a week. Our teacher said he was very good, but I didn't think so. I liked her voice much better. She didn't know how to judge herself. Just like my friend Fanny's father, who was a well-to-do farmer. He had a big batch of girls and only one boy. One day Fanny told me that her mother had had another baby girl. Her father was so disappointed that he didn't talk to his wife for several days. I explained to her that it was necessary to have a bull so a cow could have a calf. The seed the male gave the female determined what came out of the cow's belly. (Men aren't always right, even though my papa was.) A woman teacher could be just as wrong about singing as Fanny's father was about his disappointment. I liked to hear her sing; she sang like Mama.

Animals were giving birth all around us on the farm: chicks, calves and puppies. One day Dr. Hoffman met us kids walking home from school. He stopped his car and told one of the girls that she had a new baby brother. When he had left, she told us that her mother had said Dr. Hoffman would be bringing a baby to their home in the black bag that he carried. He had just delivered that baby!

In order to get home in a hurry, she started to walk fast, but I stopped her to tell her the truth about babies. I told her that I had seen pictures of an odd shape growing in a mother's stomach until it became a baby and was born. The pictures were in the medical book Papa had purchased long

Before Modern Conveniences 133

ago when he was a student at the Work People's College. She hesitated and stammered, "My mama doesn't lie!" I knew the truth so I shouted, "Pictures don't lie!" She became so upset that she ran ahead crying. Books were more accurate because they were used in schools. We didn't only learn from books in class. We were encouraged to use the school library also.

When we got home that afternoon, Helvi tattled on me. "While you are right about babies, Miriami, you must never contradict what anyone's mother has said," Mama lectured. "Having babies is such a personal matter that parents like to explain those things to their children in their own way." (But she hadn't explained anything to me and her sister in Astoria long ago had only confused me by talking about birds, bees and flowers. Papa's medical book with pictures had explained where babies come from!)

Helvi snickered and whispered as she passed me to take off her school clothes, "I told you so." She never stuck her neck out. That was the kind of person she was. Everybody was different and I thought I had a right to say what I knew was the truth. Since I didn't say anything, Mama thought I had learned my lesson. Instead, I hurriedly drank my milk and ate a slice of cardamom biscuit in silence. I wanted to play with my dog and do part of my evening chores by filling the wood box with his help. My dog brought a chunk of wood. He hadn't forgotten what I had taught him when he was a puppy! He was a good student. I wondered if I might be a teacher of kids as well as dogs.

That set me thinking about learning outside of class. Our school library was located in a small room where the stairs turned. I liked to look at all the books on the shelves, especially the colorful covers. I liked to read books about horses. Black Beauty was one of my favorites. I also liked to read Jack London's books about dogs and wolves up in the north country. Sometimes we could hear wild animals howl on Butte Hill; Papa said they were coyotes. They howled for food or for mates during certain seasons. I didn't know which, but they never came to any of the farms; they stayed in the woods near where they lived.

Wolves and coyotes liked to stay with their own kind, just like people. Although the Finns disagreed about politics, religion and how to operate the co-op, they got along better with each other than with people who spoke English. Since the Indians did not understand English, perhaps that was one of the reasons they didn't like to have white people living with them on their land. Swedes and Norwegians were not sure if Finns were Scandinavians and Scandinavians were white people. Indians thought Finns were white also! Not all grown-up people thought the way others did; that's when they got mad and fought each other. It was called a war. Papa said that wild animals also fought each other, usually over

Before Modern Conveniences

territory. Animals didn't have public schools like people had where they were taught to get along with one another rather than hate or fight.

School was interesting in the sixth and seventh grades because we had geography and history. I liked to imagine I was traveling all over the world meeting famous people. I had learned a lot about history and European people from speakers at the Finn hall. Those lectures were like the history and geography we studied at school. I felt like a traveler going from one country to another, following the teacher while studying mountains, rivers and cities, as well as meeting kings, queens and rulers with stories of their past. Neither we nor the teacher talked in any of the languages of the countries we studied. That would have made history more interesting.

Traveling all over the world made me think of walking and my feet. Walking reminded me of our cows. Their hooves parted when they moved. I had toes that did not part like hard cow's hooves, which could step on anything. When I walked barefoot on gravel, dirt, or the stubble of a newly cut hayfield, I felt what was underneath my feet and toes. I decided when I was grown up I would spend my vacations traveling around the world, not barefoot as I did now, but like a vagabond with shoes on my feet and a knapsack on my back. Mama didn't like to hear about my plans to be a vagabond and see the world. We really were different! Papa also thought life wouldn't be wonderful without a home to return to. I hadn't thought of that. I still liked history and geography. It was make-believe travel.

Another good assignment in the seventh grade was to give an oral report of what we wanted to be when we grew up. The idea was to teach us to speak up in front of a group so we would be able to do the same later in life. That's what people were supposed to do in a democracy. Papa practiced it a lot at the Finn hall, as did the other men. Women had opinions, too, but they only talked at home with their husbands about community matters.

I had a difficult time deciding what to tell the class. I no longer wanted to be a vagabond and see the world. Papa had changed my mind; I had to have a home to come back to! Then I thought I would become an Olympic runner and win a blue ribbon. I was proud of the blue ribbon I had won in the 100-yard dash at the county track meet the previous year. Both Mama and Papa said I couldn't make a living from a blue ribbon. One got prestige, but that wasn't edible.

Then I remembered: I would become a sculptor! When very young, I had carved a beautiful, muscular prancing horse! When I mentioned that to Mama, she looked at me with a surprised expression and said, "Mirri, I burned the stick you had been trying to carve with a carpenter's file." Putting her arm around my shoulders, she continued, "You had scratched it with the file, but it honestly didn't look like anything. That's why I burned it with the other trash when we were building our house." Seeing my expression, Papa cut in at this moment and said that I was possessed with an unusual imagination, but it was a good thing to have. I was pleased with what Papa said. After all, I was good at something even if I hadn't decided yet what I wanted to be later in life.

Before I had made up my mind as to a career, I was surprised when my friend Fanny told the class she wanted to be a movie star. She was as skinny as I, but her brown eyes and long eyelashes were beautiful. Her dark eyelashes tilted upwards. She didn't look like the rest of us Finnish kids. My eyelashes were skimpy, maybe because I used to get those sticky red bumps called sties that clung to my eyelids for weeks at a time. Poetry readers at the Finn hall said one could see the soul of a person through the eyes. Not true! I used my eyes just to see objects and to read. Nobody was going to see what I really was inside unless I told them! Besides, who would care to look into my eyes, since they weren't framed with long, dark, curled lashes? Fanny's desire to be a movie star was really different from most of my classmates who wanted to be farmers or housewives.

I was sensible enough to know that I couldn't ever be as glamorous as a movie star, but I wanted to be different than everyone else in the class. Then I realized how often I had thought of being a teacher. (That was long before I had even gone to school!) Being a teacher would be better than being a farmer's wife like Mama. I understood her now. She couldn't help being bossy; she was a mother. But teachers could control many children in a class by instructing them! That was better because it was teaching.

After carefully thinking of my choice of career, I told the family what I had chosen for my oral report. Both Papa and Mama were pleased. They thought being a teacher was the best possible job one could have, since being educated made democracy work. But Mama said that was only partially true. Common sense helped also, she said. Papa nodded in agreement. With the approval of both Mama and Papa, my former fantasies were gone. I knew what I wanted to do and decided not to spend time on fantasies anymore.

I got an A for my oral report. That was as good as being applauded after my poetry recitations at the Finn hall.

9

The Finn Hall: Our Community Center

Shortly before construction of the first Finn hall was finished, it was completely destroyed by fire. Papa was chosen to use the $400 insurance money to purchase the lumber for a new building that was to be built on another piece of property donated by a farmer. The reason Papa was chosen to do this important job was because he was one of two Finns who was a citizen. Although we spoke only Finnish at home, everyone knew he could understand and speak some English.

. Papa took a barge in Woodland that was anchored at Caples Landing near the junction of the Lewis and Columbia Rivers. He purchased the lumber from the Clark and Wilson mill on the Oregon side. When the lumber was delivered, several farmers with teams of horses hauled the lumber to the building site. With a bid of $135, the Tuisku brothers constructed the new hall. Although the bid was considered high, none of the other farmers had bid because they were too busy clearing their land or plowing what had been cleared. The Tuiskus were considered well-off because they had paid cash for their farm so they were free to take on the contract.

Sometime after the building was completed, a picnic at a nearby creek was planned. There were so many people there that it looked as if the world had settled next to that slow-moving clear creek. Food was set on makeshift tables. Eating and visiting went on immediately. After a while games were organized. A man was in charge of racing. He asked for girls between the ages of six and eight to line up. I liked running. I was among the first to dash to the starting place but was told I was too young. I knew that! They just didn't know how fast I could run. Age had nothing to do with one's ability to run. Several old women tried to talk me out of racing, but I wouldn't move. When the gong struck, I plunged on ahead of the others and immediately my nose scraped the pebbles on the ground. Somebody had tripped me! I got up immediately. The other runners were reaching the finish line. I was stunned. The tip of my nose hurt, but I didn't cry. Only babies cried.

A nice lady came over to me and offered me a bag of the hard colored candy from the co-op that was given to all who took part in the race. I refused to take it because I had not earned it. She didn't understand me. She coaxed and coaxed. I just stomped my foot and said, "I don't want candy." (I didn't tell her that I only wanted to be the winner in the race.) I couldn't help it if somebody with bigger feet and longer legs had got in my way. When I had fallen on other occasions and bruised my nose, in order to comfort me, Mama had said, "Eyes see danger ahead; the poor nose is hurt instead." My nose now felt the truth of that saying.

There was so much going on that soon nobody paid attention to my scratched nose and hurt feelings. I was lost in the crowd. Even Papa and Mama stood around talking to others. Helvi hung around with the older girls and didn't want me to tag around with her so I spent the time eating and watching the sack races. I picked food from the tables, just as the other kids were doing. I didn't even think of the candy I might have won. Eating kept me busy.

One winter a Christmas party was held at the hall. A huge Douglas fir tree stood in the corner. It was decorated with real candles inserted in holders and attached to the branches with clothespins. White popcorn and red cranberry chains spiralled around the tree. The popcorn and cranberries came from the co-op as a gift; women whose husbands were on the board of directors had made them into chains. The other decoration was shredded cotton balls. They were strewn willy-nilly on the branches of the tree, like wind-blown snow. All the families from Butte Hill and the other hills around the northern bank of the Lewis River and beyond were there. It was a festival of friends.

When Santa Claus distributed bags filled with candy, nuts and an orange from the co-op to us kids, my friend Riitta pointed to Santa and shouted, "That's my daddy!" I poked her, demanding, "What makes you think that's your papa?" Jumping up and down in delight, she said that her daddy had lost half his finger while working in a sawmill and Santa had half a finger missing. "That's proof!" She laughed and danced happily in front of him.

Regardless of whose papa he was, Santa pretended not to notice the clamor around him. He continued passing out the Christmas bags to us kids. I was glad that he didn't stop to smile at Riitta. (I would really have liked it if my papa had been Santa Claus.) I knew Riitta was right because I had heard people say he had lost half a finger in a sawmill accident. That type of work was more dangerous than working on a farm. We all knew Santas were make-believe characters, like the men who acted on the Finn hall stage.

Suddenly, wild clamoring ended the laughter as somebody shouted, "Fire!" A couple of shredded cotton balls had caught fire. In no time at all several men had put out the fire, surrounded the tree and blown out the candles, after which Santa handed out the remainder of the treats.

Under the tree was a large box of cards that Santa distributed in order to save the one-cent postage. Almost everybody got a Christmas card from somebody in the room. Uncle Sam didn't care; he had a lot more money than any of the farmers. As the distribution of the cards went on, it was obvious that one person had received the most cards, plus several presents. It was Alli, the daughter of the Ahlgrens. Her father was a popular man in the community. He was in charge of selecting the plays because he was a musician and an actor. He had already assigned certain people to the play, which was to be performed as soon as the characters had practiced for a couple of months.

Although Mr. Ahlgren had been a success somewhere else before coming to Woodland, his wife had wanted to come here because she had two sisters who lived on Butte Hill. Alli's mama was quite a bit older than her husband, and everybody felt sorry for her because he was known as a "ladies' man," whatever that meant. Alli was prettier than any of the little girls pictured in the Sears or Ward's catalogs. She had bright blue eyes and slightly curly blonde hair. It wasn't kinky or streaked like mine. Alli wasn't fat like my sister or skinny like me. She looked like a doll. I didn't even have a doll; Mama had given me an old teddy bear that I liked to hug when I went to bed.

After the Christmas celebration was over, the hall committee decided that in future there would be no card or gift distribution at the hall. Uncle Sam was to get all the business from the Woodland farmers. That was the way it should have been in the first place. Saving money on postage wasn't as important as good fellowship.

At home on Christmas Day I did get a present: a pair of gray woolen mittens that Mama had knitted. She gave the same to Helvi, only hers were black. She gave Papa knitted woolen stockings. She had done all that knitting at the kitchen table near the kerosene lamp after the barn work was done. She had also made a cake for herself and shared it with all of us. While enjoying the cake, Helvi and I told the story about Santa Claus that we had read in our schoolbooks. We all laughed because our chimney was too small for anyone to slide down. Besides, our mittens and Papa's stockings would have burned!

Not long after the Christmas party, we had a wonderful talent show at the hall. It was the most exciting event I had ever attended because I had a part in it. Mr. Ahlgren played the piano and the violin. The music made me feel as if I were in another world. I was lost in a world of make-believe. In between his performances, somebody read a poem and then a man from the neighboring Finnish community in Kalama gave a speech on the rights of working people in this country. By the time he had finished talking, I was on pins and needles waiting for the children's poetry competition take place.

Grown-up Finns liked poetry. I did, too, but the poem Mama had chosen for me to memorize was too short. I liked Helvi's poem better because it was longer. One chubby boy got the audience chuckling because he recited a poem about a boy being round like a barrel. (So was he.) I knew my poem wouldn't make anyone laugh. It just described what went on in everyone's home: papas waiting for mamas to put kids to sleep and papas reading the newspaper in the evenings while mamas were still working. (Papas worked with horses and heavy machinery so they got tired and needed to relax in the evenings. Putting kids to bed was not their job.)

When I got up to recite, I fidgeted, fiddled with my dress, and hung my head. I eyed the long row of buttons on my shoes and stared at my underwear bulging under my woolen stockings. I raced through the poem, mumbling in Finnish.

My little mutt, do not cry,
Daddy's sparkling star in sky.
Mama will come as soon as she can
To fetch her li'l one to slumber lan!

I heard people clapping, maybe just Mama and Papa. Even though she didn't want to, Helvi recited the poem she had memorized. She got as much applause as I did. Her poem was longer.

After the program and refreshment periods were over, everyone enjoyed dancing. Between dances, we kids slid around in the middle of the floor, bumping and jostling one another. Sometimes someone would fall. If it was a girl, we'd slide over and help brush the powder off her dress. It was the white stuff that made the floor slippery. I thought that the musicians liked to rest while we kids laughed and played on the dance floor.

Helvi didn't join us. She thought she was too grown-up to slide and scuffle. She wouldn't dance with Mama either, but I did because Papa was not a dancer. All men who didn't dance, like Papa, were said to have "preacher's legs." That's because most Lutheran preachers said dancing was wrong. I don't know why having fun was wrong, but that's what they said in the old country. (It was also reported that when people danced late on Saturday nights, they would be too tired to go to church on Sunday.) There was no church for Finns in Woodland so going to dances couldn't be wrong.

Papa usually sold admission tickets at the door. Also, during the intermission, he would hold the door open to let people into the kitchen where coffee and cardamom biscuits were served. Papa didn't play favorites. I knew that; I tried it once. He wouldn't let my friends and me push in to the front of the line. (I had tried to show off to them because their fathers weren't guarding the door.) Papa scolded me at home. He said I had no more privileges than anyone else. At school we had to line up after recess and lunch before going into class—just like the Finns insisted on lining up at the hall. It felt OK to obey.

Not all women danced. Mr. Koski, who lived further up Butte Hill Road from us, often danced the first dance with Mama because his wife didn't dance. Nobody said Mrs. Koski had "preacher's legs." Only men had them! While Mr. Koski and Mama danced, Papa was busy selling tickets at the entrance of the hall and Mrs. Koski sat on a northside bench in the hall, chatting with her sisters. None of them danced. The husbands of all three read different newspapers that were published in various parts of the United States: the West Coast, Minnesota, and way back East. The sisters had a lot to talk about; their husbands' ideas made no difference to them. They got along better than their husbands!

Getting together at someone's home after the sauna or at co-op meetings, grown-ups often raised their voices. They sounded as if they were arguing, but Papa said they were disagreeing. That was different. That was OK when you lived in a country that allowed a person to say what he thought, Papa explained.

The best part of Finn hall activities was when I got to dance with Mama. She taught me how by telling me to stand with one foot on each of her shoes. That way I felt what her feet were doing. It worked, I think, because soon she let me put my feet on the floor. Helvi said I still couldn't dance. She said I hopped as fast as my feet would go just to keep out of Mama's way. Mama had tried to get her to dance, but she wouldn't. Helvi just watched others dance and eventually learned.

I didn't think watching was a good way to learn anything. I liked doing. I wasn't a watcher like Helvi. Many sisters don't look alike. That's why Helvi and I were different. I wondered whether I'd have been different from a brother, if I'd had one. If he'd have danced with me, that would have been really special! Most brothers at the hall didn't dance with their sisters. They chose a neighbor girl. That was odd. I felt sure my brother would have liked to dance with me.

The biggest event every year was the May Day celebration at the hall. That's when there were many speeches. Some were against the revolution in Russia and some thought that any change from the days of the czar's rule was better for Finland. One speaker said the best way to create good conditions for working people in this country was by political action and another said only unions could accomplish that. Grown-ups liked to hear long speeches; that's how they learned something new. They read only one newspaper at home, but at the hall they heard everyone's opinions.

Mama was a sharecropper's daughter in Finland so she never went to school, not even for one day. The village priest taught her to read after her work was done in the evening. She was proud of having passed confirmation with kids who had taken classes during the day! She had a motto: one had to learn something new every day. That was why she liked to listen to all those speakers. Some influenced her and she changed her mind, sometimes even disagreeing with Papa. That was when I felt she was wrong. She hadn't read books like Papa had when he attended the Work People's College.

Getting an education for their kids was one of the reasons some people came to America. Only the wealthy could afford an education in Finland. Nevertheless, everyone in Finland could read because the church taught people to read the Bible. That was good, but not as good as going to a public school here.

Special activities took place during the strawberry season. Woodland and Kalama Finns took turns having strawberry dances during the berry harvest. Everybody went, young and old. When the men weren't dancing, they talked about their berry crops and the market. We often danced until one in the morning, went home, slept a few hours and got up in time to be in the fields at six.

Strawberries ripened even on Sundays. One of our pickers didn't want to work on Sunday; she said it was a day of rest. Mama told her that God ripened berries every single day so if she refused to pick, it would not be according to nature, which was also God's plan. I knew Mama believed it was a waste to let ripened berries rot. I also knew it didn't matter what one believed; rotten berries were a waste and that was not good. Our reluctant picker changed her mind. She worked every day.

I heard Papa tell Mama jokingly that maybe her argument about waste did not persuade the picker to work. He thought his promise did the trick. He had said he would pay an extra quarter cent a pound on all berries picked if the pickers worked every day during the entire season. If they didn't, they wouldn't get that money. I worked daily, rain or shine as well as Sundays, to get my bonus. That was my job and I did it like all the other pickers who weren't members of our family. Mama and Papa did not argue who was right. They were satisfied the berries were picked before they rotted in the fields.

At one of the strawberry dances the hall was so full of people dancing that one couldn't see across the hall. Even the benches were almost empty! I was dancing with Wilho, the boy who had "mooned" me long ago. Although I didn't like him, he was an excellent dancer and that was what counted on the dance floor. I heard he told "dirty" jokes because he had been adopted and learned about sex the "hard" way by hearing his parents talk. Mama said one shouldn't believe everything one heard; it was only gossip. Wilho whirled me around so fast that somebody bumped into him and down he fell to the dance floor with me following! I jumped to my feet and pulled him up at the same time. It was easy; he was as skinny as I. Although embarrassed, we just started dancing again as if nothing had happened.

When the music stopped, I left him before he was able to escort me to where we girls stood as a group in one corner of the hall. I crept up to Helvi and asked if she'd seen me fall down. "Where? Here?" She was surprised. I didn't know what to say. I only nodded in reply. "Nobody was watching you, Mirri," she said. "Everybody was busy picking their way around the dance floor," she assured me. Sisters were nice, I thought, except when we disagreed. Helvi was right because nobody made fun of my falling with Wilho. Other guys asked me to dance that evening, but not Wilho. I was glad of that.

At some of the other dances, when there weren't so many people, we girls sometimes danced together if a guy came towards us with whom we didn't want to dance. Then we danced around the hall and came close to the boys' corner. That was when two bashful boys would break us up and ask us to dance. It worked every time. As long as they could dance, it didn't matter if they were too bashful to talk. It was dancing that was important.

We girls were better dancers than the boys. We had to adjust our steps to the guys'! Every boy had a different way of keeping up with the music. Some waltzed, turned, or sidestepped clumsily. We had to match our feet to theirs even if they weren't keeping step with the music. Although they'd danced for many years, those fellows just went through the same routine regardless of the music. They were the guys that Riitta and I were usually able to avoid by dancing together before they reached us.

At one of the dances during strawberry season, a girl from Portland who'd come to Woodland to pick berries refused to dance with Otto. Otto was very tall and his face was covered with eczema, which made him look awful. He looked like a clown, but none of us local girls cared about his looks because he was the best dancer in the world. We could even carry on a conversation with him and not be concerned about our feet. His whole body kept time exactly with the tempo of the music. I liked dancing and talking at the same time and it was nice to press my cheek against his chest because it smelled of cigarettes. He carried the packet in his shirt pocket.

Many boys smoked. Several offered me a cigarette, which I would take home with me. I wrote the boy's name in ink on the cigarette and put it in a little box. Riitta and I had a contest to see who would get the most cigarettes from boys. Not one of us girls smoked. A bad habit like that was OK for boys but not for girls.

I liked the smell of cigarette smoke on boys' clothes; it smelled almost like Papa's, but different. Papa's smell came from a pipe. He said the smoke dried the drip from his nose. Mama didn't think it worked because his nose still dripped even after smoking for years and years. The tobacco that Papa put into his pipe came from a metal container he carried in his shirt pocket.

Otto was surprised when the girl turned him down. Since I was sitting next to her, he asked me to dance. I jumped up, of course. I thought Otto was hurt because the Portland girl was so pretty and she wore a store-bought dress. Our mamas made our dresses from a pattern someone had cut out from a newspaper. Although our dresses were made from the same home-made pattern, they didn't look alike because either the material, the color or the design of the cloth was different. The clerk at the co-op knew from which bolt of cloth the Butte Hill mothers had bought. She was smart that way. That's why everybody liked her. She had worked there as long as I could remember and she knew everyone's name.

Any dress Mama made for me was fine just as long as it wasn't red. I didn't like red because it matched the pimples that had started to pop up on my cheeks. Helvi never had pimples when she was growing up, but she was sort of chubby. It was OK for me to say that, but I got mad when I heard a girl say that Helvi was fat. I yelled right back and told her she needed to have her eyes examined. My sister was not a sack of bones like she and I were. That shut her up. Helvi told me it was nice that I talked back to the girl but thought I should not have yelled. Knowing I would get into trouble, she didn't tell Mama that I had.

Papa was annoyed at me when I sassed Mama one day just when they were getting ready to have coffee. I had raised my voice and said something like, "Do you always have to tell me what to do?" That hit Papa the wrong way. He ordered me to go out and get a switch. I couldn't believe what he said so I stood there, shocked. He repeated the order. I knew then he meant business so I turned and left the room. I went to the area beyond the barn where there were trees and stayed outdoors as long as I dared. When I returned, Papa asked for the switch. I stood there in front of him for a long time. He didn't say a word. I had never been spanked with a switch before so I was really afraid. Speaking slowly, he finally said that my conscience must have told me it was wrong to talk in that tone to Mama. He wouldn't spank me now, but there was going to be no second chance. I was never spanked; I was always careful what I said when Papa was around.

Several years previously we had had Finnish language classes at the hall, but it didn't last long because one of the teachers spent a lot of time talking about the evils of industrialization. The other teacher spoke about the Russian revolution. I understood Finnish, but I wanted to write Finnish so I just waited for their speeches to end. Mama said I could learn more Finnish by continuing to read to them in the evenings and by writing for the children's corner in the women's newspaper, as well as writing to my cousin in Finland. As time went by, fewer and fewer of us kids went to the language classes. Besides, there was real work to be done on the farms.

The athletic club wasn't successful either. Helvi and I went to several meetings where an adult would lead us in calisthenics. Most of the farmers had been miners who needed athletic clubs to get fresh air in the coal country. Attendance at the club gatherings dwindled little by little for we had plenty of fresh air on the hillsides. Besides, we had calisthenics at school where it was a relief from sitting so long in a classroom.

Shortly after the hall was built, the Finns decided to establish a library and have it located at the hall. The grown-ups started to call the hall group the *Kirjalisuus Seura*, which meant literary society. Papa donated all of his books to the library, including the medical book showing how a fetus grew into a baby. Papa kept only a Finnish-English dictionary and one English-Finnish dictionary. He had his name stamped on the inside cover of each; that's how proud he was of having those dictionaries.

Before Modern Conveniences

Whenever Papa wanted to correct the business letters he made me write, he would pick up the Finnish-English dictionary and suggest a better word; I learned a lot doing that. I had a little black English dictionary, but it was at school. Some kids thought it was a Bible! It was no wonder they thought so because I liked to talk about religion and politics just like grown-ups did.

The only library Woodland had was the one at school so the Finns had a public library before the town of Woodland had one! My parents checked out books only during the winter when they didn't have so much outside farm work. Mama checked out a novel in Finnish from the hall library and I read it out loud in the evenings while Helvi did her schoolwork. The book was about seven brothers who were unruly and got into a lot of mischief. As time went on, they learned how to behave.

Papa did not read the newspaper when I struggled through the book. Reading it was more difficult than reading the articles we kids wrote for the children's corner of the women's monthly newspaper. Helvi refused to read or write Finnish so she didn't pay any attention to me; that was because sisters were different. But Mama and Papa listened closely as I read. They even corrected my pronunciation. That was OK. If I went to Finland, I could talk like a Finlander.

When the hall stage was constructed, there was a lot of talk about having paid $40 to the man who had painted the drop curtain. The painting was of a woodland scene in Finland. It was the only picture I had ever seen of the countryside my parents came from. There wasn't a single Douglas fir on the canvas! Some people did not like giving the contract to the painter whose parents seldom came to the hall except when the co-op held its semi-annual and annual meetings. Most everybody agreed, however, that an artist was worth that much money. Besides, he was the only man in the community who could paint so people quit griping and enjoyed the scenery.

Co-op meetings were interesting. Papa was chosen to be on the executive board once in a while. It was an honor to be on the board so competition was keen. Papa was once involved in a disagreement as to whether a contract should be given to replace a wooden floor that had rotted in the dry goods section. He wanted a concrete floor that would last a long time. A comment was made that liberals like Papa were always ready to spend more public money than necessary. The contract was put out for bids. It turned out that a concrete floor would cost $10 more than a wooden one. The board decided to accept the more expensive bid since it would save money in the long run. Papa called it "long-range vision," like buying books, reading and learning from them.

Before Modern Conveniences

Papa had other troubles while on the co-op executive board. I never found out what the problem was because Papa and Mama only whispered about it in bed. One day Papa went to town; he returned in the afternoon and slowly drank his coffee while Mama asked him about shopping at the English store across the street from the co-op.

What was going on? I was puzzled. I heard Papa mumble that he had made a terrible mistake getting so angry as to quit shopping at the co-op, the store in which he was a shareholder. His voice sunk into silence. Mama didn't sympathize with him. Instead she reminded him, "I told you not to get so angry." (Mama should have told Papa that it was courageous to admit a mistake because that's what she always told me!) She ordered, "Go to the next board meeting. Stay calm." Her final bit of advice to Papa was, "Don't say you shopped across the street!" After a pause, Mama sighed. "Now you know how others feel when their suggestions aren't adopted." Without replying, Papa drank his coffee. That ended the matter. They never talked about it again.

We kids liked to attend the co-op meetings. The men sat in the center of the hall, while women lined the benches on either side or worked in the kitchen. I liked listening to the discussions on the profit and loss statement and operating expenses. My friend Fanny's daddy wasn't a full-blooded Finn but an Estonian who spoke Finnish with an odd accent, maybe like Papa spoke English. (Since he never spoke English at home or around us, I didn't know if he had an accent.) People who spoke with an accent sounded as if they were pronouncing misspelled words.

Fanny's daddy knew bookkeeping because he had a big herd of cows and lots of kids to milk them. He didn't even have a mortgage! Papa had taken bookkeeping at the Work People's College so the two men sometimes disagreed about the financial condition of the co-op. I learned that everyone had the same influence—one vote—in a cooperative regardless of the number of shares a person owned. A cooperative was like a democracy, but it didn't sound like that at the meetings. Fanny's daddy was rich and that meant he was a powerhouse at all the meetings. I could tell he was respected. When the discussion went back and forth endlessly, I got all mixed up so I enjoyed my usual fantasies, which kept me occupied until the lunch break.

When roused from my daydreams, the wait for the break was worthwhile. We had sandwiches made from store-bought white bread as well as whole wheat. They tasted better than what we ate at home. Most of us kids took one of each, but nobody cared. Some sandwiches had a slice of Tillamook cheese and others had ham. In addition, we were

Before Modern Conveniences

served free soda pop. I always chose strawberry. What a treat! We kids gathered together chattering and gobbling down the sandwiches between gulps of soda pop. The store was profitable. It provided us with those good refreshments! Sometimes there were a few sandwiches left when the meeting resumed. We took care of that in true cooperative spirit: we shared.

An animated discussion once took place at a hall meeting about the bird droppings on the windows of the hall. The argument was not between groups of men like at the co-op meetings; it was between the men and the women. This time I could understand everything that was said. It was the only time women actually spoke up at hall meetings! They let the men know they did not want the swallows nesting under the eaves. There were at least 50 nests there, the length of the hall. The birds carried clay from the Lewis riverbank nearby, placed the clay there and worked their nests into shape with their beaks. The droppings painted the windows with odd shapes so one couldn't see the Lewis River clearly. Since the women had spent several hours cleaning the mess from the windows, they demanded the men get rid of the nests.

It was interesting to hear Papa and several other men talk about the useful work swallows did. They devoured insects! Thus the men appreciated the birds. Insects did damage to crops, but the droppings on the windows only obscured the view of the river. After the eggs hatched, the new brood would fly away. That was when the women could clean the windows, but not now!

One after the other, the women spoke. They didn't care about the useful work the swallows did. Windows were made so people could look outside and see nature as it really was. They spoke on a subject which they felt was very important; cleanliness was next to godliness! They hadn't come to America to look at windows covered with bird s**t!

Although they weren't citizens, the women spoke from experience. One woman said if the men didn't get rid of the nests, she would never wash the windows in her home. A wave of nodding heads followed that remark and throughout the hall there was a murmur of agreement from the women.

Finally, the men couldn't take it anymore. They said they'd get ladders and knock down the nests. The women agreed to wash the windows before the next event at the hall. To this day I don't know where the swallows went to lay their eggs. I felt sorry for the birds. How were they to know that people didn't want them to nest under the eaves of our hall?

Despite the meetings, programs, disagreements, hurt feelings, groups of special friendships, and the activities among the different cliques and groups, I still had not learned what was right and what was wrong. The disagreement about bird droppings on the window showed that agreement came after a lot of talk. When I grew up, I knew I'd leave home like the birds, but I had no idea of where I'd go.

I had had a part in a play called *The Shoemaker's Shack*. I liked my part because I was the bossy wife of a shoemaker. It was an easy role because all I had to do was act like Mama. The play was in Finnish because that was the language all the farmers understood. Various socio-political groups also put on plays. Sometimes we went to all the events at the hall. Other times my parents said they wouldn't support this or that. When we went, I was often asked to go around collecting money for some worthwhile cause like a strike in the garment industry back East or someone's release from jail for having been involved in a labor dispute. I liked doing that. Helping the underdog was good citizenship. As I went around from man to man, he wrote his name on the collection list and the amount he contributed. That way nobody could steal any money that was donated. All monies were sent to the national office of the organization through the United States post office in town. Papa did that because he spoke English.

We also collected money when someone got married. A committee of three best friends would comb separate areas of the Finnish community for donations. The closest friends would usually donate one dollar or more; neighbors and acquaintances, 50 cents; others who didn't like the people for one reason or another would donate 25 cents simply because they wanted to attend the wedding dance.

Those events were as much fun as the strawberry dances because there was no other program other than the wedding march where everybody except the very old joined in. The committee usually purchased a set of silver-plated forks, knives and spoons for the couple. The money that was collected also paid for the musicians and the rest was given to the couple. The gift was put on the dance floor next to the stage so everybody could see it.

Before the dancing, a wedding march took place, which was led by a couple familiar with the routine. The newlyweds followed them and everybody who had a partner joined the march, which was like a drill with all kinds of twists and turns. When the music stopped, people in the line would take their turn greeting the couple and take a peek at the gift. It was interesting to find out whether the bride or groom would deliver the thank-you speech in Finnish. Sometimes one could no longer speak Finnish fluently, so the other would. The other then spoke in English as some *toiskieliset* (outsiders) were occasionally present. Our parents didn't want them to feel uncomfortable among us Finns as they had been made to feel on arriving in this country.

The musicians and wedding couple had refreshments first. As soon as the musicians had had their coffee, they went up on stage and played. There were so many people present that it took a long time before everyone could be served refreshments in the kitchen. The dancing went on until one in the morning.

Other social activities at the hall included evenings of singing, piano music, violin solos, poetry and speeches. Several years earlier Helvi's boyfriend's parents in Kalama had taken as their ward an orphan boy from Montana. His name was Jeff. His father had died in a Butte mine explosion. Sometime later his mother died in the flu epidemic. His aunt had just started to work in a boarding house and didn't have time to take care of him. She had recently written to Jeff's caretakers in Kalama asking them to allow him to return to Montana to live with her since her husband had been stabbed in the stomach by a drunken man as they were leaving the Temperance Hall in Butte. He had died on the way to the hospital. Jeff's aunt believed her nephew would be able to get a good job in the mine since he had graduated from the eighth grade. Much as he liked his life now, Jeff said he was obligated to go.

Jeff always accompanied Helvi's boyfriend when he came to pick her up to go to the hall. Naturally, I went along, so Jeff and I had become good friends over the years. Jeff was a terrific dancer, just as good as Otto but not as tall. Jeff was only a couple of inches taller than I was. We danced together a lot. Jeff smoked cigarettes. I liked the tobacco smell on his clothes. It wafted in the air as we danced a lively schottische and then a dignified waltz. He never stepped on my toes because we both moved in rhythm with the music. We were meant for each other as dancing partners, but not for long.

At a dance early in December Jeff told me he was definitely going to his aunt's home in Butte, Montana, the Big Sky State. She needed him. Jeff said he was sorry he couldn't be here for my thirteenth birthday. He told me he would write every week and I promised I would do the same.

After each dance ended, we stood together and held hands. Nobody else could get me to dance and I felt he didn't want to get another girl! We smiled at each other. Suddenly he let go of my hand and hugged me gently while waiting for the next dance to start. I had never felt like this before. I realized Jeff was my boyfriend! It was a good feeling. I was happy to be a girl.

10

I'm a Teenager!

When we went to school on the thirteenth, Mama reminded us to hurry home. Naturally we would: it was my birthday! There would be the usual cake and cambric tea for us. Although they kept my legs warm, I hoped Mama wouldn't give me another pair of long knitted woolen stockings. I had outgrown them. Teenagers shouldn't have to dress like kids. With the weather cold and a layer of snow on the road, we didn't dawdle and chatter as usual on the climb up Butte Hill.

Heavy snow covered the hillsides. The boughs of the Douglas fir trees were bent in graceful arches and rabbit tracks broke the smoothness of the snow in spots beside the road. Brown tracks of horses' hooves and deep ruts of wagon wheels revealed that Papa had returned home from town. We looked into the mailbox, but it was empty. Papa had picked up the mail.

After Papa had unharnessed the horses and deposited the sacks of chicken feed and grain for the cows, he entered the house carrying a small bag of flour, some groceries and the mail. He stared at me and turned slowly to Mama, asking, "Coffee?" Despite the weather, she had expected Papa to arrive at the usual time so the coffee was ready for him. Papa brightened and in measured tones proposed that Helvi and I sit at the table and have coffee! Helvi and I looked at each other: the invitation was out of the ordinary.

We looked at Papa as he fingered a letter in his hand. Could he have forgotten that we were "earning" one dollar every year for not drinking coffee daily?! Something was bothering him if he was suddenly changing, without an explanation, a custom that had lasted so many years. Helvi quickly pushed another chair up to the table. She was eager to please. However, Papa's eyes were riveted on me as he said, "Come, Mirri, sit here next to me." That was really unusual! I was mystified. Mama filled our cups.

Papa poured coffee from his cup into his saucer, raised it to his lips and sipped as if he was thinking of something else. His other hand held the letter, which he laid face down on the table. He placed a cube of sugar on his tongue. In slow motion he raised the saucer to his mouth and took another sip. Then he hurriedly emptied the saucer and placed it on the table.

"I want all of you to know what I heard at the store while waiting for Lempi to fill the order," Papa began in a solemn manner. After a pause, he added, "A man from Kalama told me that Jeff's aunt in Montana had sent a telegram that Jeff had died in a cave-in at the mine on his second day in the job."

I jumped up and screamed, "Don't believe everything you hear!" Searching for something to bolster my disbelief, I cried, "You've told me many times not to repeat everything that somebody has said!" I ran off to the bedroom, threw myself on the bed and sobbed.

After some time I realized that there was total silence in the kitchen. Perhaps there was something else. There was that letter. Maybe it was for me! Maybe it was from Jeff! I felt something was wrong because nobody was talking. I wiped

Before Modern Conveniences   165

the tears from my eyes and entered the kitchen. I wasn't a child anymore. I was a full-grown teenager. I could face any kind of problem like a grown-up. I saw Papa tapping the letter on the table as if he was nervous. He didn't say anything, just handed it to me. It was from Jeff!! I had received the letter he had promised to send me and it had arrived on my birthday!

With eager fingers, I tore the envelope open and read.

Dear Mirri,
This was my first day on the job. I worked 10 hours in the cold and damp mine, which wasn't easy. I'm very tired. When I get my first paycheck, I'll give half to my aunt for my room and board and with the other half will buy you a Christmas present. I'm worn out. Going to bed.
Your special friend,
Jeff

P.S. See this X? That's my birthday gift to you.

The days when I had to sing for the letters I received were long gone. It was a real joy and pleasure to realize Jeff had written to me the very first day he had worked! Instead of my lips singing, my heart sang. Jeff was only 15 years old and was doing a man's job! I was happy; Jeff was alive!

While watching me searchingly, Papa took something from his pocket as he said, "Jeff's death in a cave-in is no gossip," and handed a Western Union telegram to me. He sighed. "It was left at the co-op by Jeff's friends in Kalama with instructions to give it to you, Mirri." As if to console me, he murmured, "Cave-ins happened several times when I worked underground." A dry cough and another sigh revealed that Papa was deeply affected. I read the telegram and pressed it to my chest.

This shattering news from the Big Sky State was hard to accept. I knew it was reality, not like the fantasies I had enjoyed all my life. I heard Papa murmur that such is life: taking the bad with the good. He was talking to me like he talked to grown-ups! I raised my head and saw Helvi enjoying her coffee. I realized we were both teenagers now, halfway along the road to becoming adults and had the privilege of having coffee during the afternoon break. That was nice.

"Look, it's stopped snowing," remarked Helvi. It had happened quickly. The heavy snow-laden clouds had blown away and more light appeared for us at the table. Mama whipped out a handkerchief and wiped the moisture from my cheeks.

Without reading the headlines, Papa had placed his Finnish newspaper aside. He cleared his throat; he had something else to reveal to us. "There are many problems in the world that we can't do anything about at this time, but..." With a sudden twinkle in his eyes, he quickly added, "I heard some good news in town today." His voice matched the light in his eyes. "The Vancouver cooperative cannery has sold all the strawberries we sent them this summer at a good price so we'll be getting a big check before Christmas." Taking a deep breath, he continued, "We'll have enough money to buy galvanized pipes to bring water to the porch." With a pleased look at Mama, he added, "That will be a practical Christmas present for you." Mama smiled.

Seizing the good news right away, Helvi suggested that she would like to splurge and make a golden cake using half a dozen eggs. With a new challenging look at Mama, she asked, "We can afford to use that many eggs now, can't we?" Mama nodded and said, "We'll have a real party tonight when we return from the barn."

While Mama and I were changing into our barn clothes, Papa remarked that there was going to be a frost so he'd bet-

Before Modern Conveniences

ter bring the bucket of water from the porch into the house. Opening the door, he shouted, "Mirri, look what's here!" With his tail wagging and a chunk of wood on the doorstep, there stood Shepy! "You taught your dog well," Papa declared in a complimentary tone.

Shep had waited long enough to do our evening chore and had done his part to remind me of it. I bent down and scratched the back of his ears. "Let's get more wood, Shepy! The wood box needs to be filled." He ran ahead. I enjoyed his company, especially now.

When our task was finished, Mama told Helvi that when the cake was in the oven she should make *kala mojakka* (fish chowder). She had brought the chunk of salted fish from the cellar and it was already washed and ready for slicing. "Cut up the larger dry onion in the pantry to boil with the peeled potatoes," Mama advised. Helvi replied with a grin, "Slicing it will make me get tears in my eyes like—" I interrupted, shouting, "That's not the same as me!" As soon as that came out of my mouth, Mama suggested, "Throw extra peppercorns in to flavor the chowder for Mirri. She likes the taste." Mama was a peacemaker. That was OK.

Evening chores began at dusk with Papa carrying a lantern and a bucket of hot water to the milk house. Beside him, Mama sang as the frozen snow crackled under their feet. Stars popped out one by one; it was almost like the starlit night long ago when Mama, Helvi and I had sat on a plank and enjoyed the see-saw on the sawhorse while Mama sang.

Tonight, all those years later, the same stars sparkled all over the world. They sparkled on those who saw them as well as on those who couldn't. I felt I was momentarily with Jeff. I knew that the stars in the Big Sky State sparkled on Jeff's grave like the ones that lit our present evening trek to the barn. I wiped a new tear that had fallen to keep it from freezing. Stars were forever. The sky had not fallen.

SUGGESTED TOPICS FOR THOUGHT, DISCUSSION OR WRITTEN ASSIGNMENT

1. What do you think of a mother leaving her four-year-old alone while she goes on an important errand? Would a mother today do likewise? Explain.

2. Why was the food limited? Did it lack any basic nutritional element? In what way were children involved in preparing or serving food?

3. What health practice was unusual? How about massage therapy today?

4. Was there a difference in chores and work? Explain.

5. Why were visitors appreciated?

6. How has the delivery of United States mail changed in relation to getting news? Do you prefer e-mail to written letters? Why or why not?

7. Are group games as a form of relaxation as popular today or has competition become more important? Explain.

8. Are children from other countries today any different that those of European immigrants at the turn of the century? What was the attitude of Miriami's parents about

getting an education and at the same time maintinaing their own ethnic heritage?

9. Do immigrants from other countries tend to have gathering places where they prefer to associate while adjusting to our ways of living? Do you think that is OK? Why or why not?

10. Describe the reaction of the family members to Miriami's news in the last chapter. What does the ending mean?

Printed in the United States
19570LVS00004B/295-342